Library of Shakespearean Biography and Criticism

I. PRIMARY REFERENCE WORKS ON SHAKESPEARE

II. CRITICISM AND INTERPRETATION

- A. Textual Treatises, Commentaries
- B. Treatment of Specal Subjects
- C. Dramatic and Literary Art in Shakespeare

III. SHAKESPEARE AND HIS TIME

- A. General Treatises. Biography
- B. The Age of Shakespeare
- C. Authorship

Library of Shakespearean Biography and Criticism

Series II, Part C

SHAKESPEARE PLAYS
AND PAGEANTS

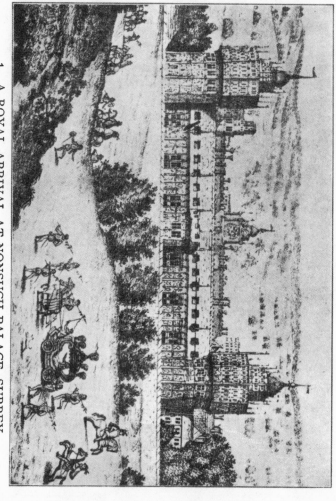

1. A ROYAL ARRIVAL AT NONSUCH PALACE, SURREY.

Library of Shakespearean Biography and Criticism

A BOOK FOR SHAKESPEARE PLAYS AND PAGEANTS

A Treasury of Elizabethan and Shakespearean Detail for Producers, Stage Managers, Actors, Artists and Students.

BY

ORIE LATHAM HATCHER

Illustrated with nearly 200 Pictures and Portraits, mostly from Contemporary Sources.

BOOKS FOR LIBRARIES PRESS
FREEPORT, NEW YORK

First Published 1916
Reprinted 1970

822.33

XH

69428

March, 1970

STANDARD BOOK NUMBER:
8369-5258-8

LIBRARY OF CONGRESS CATALOG CARD NUMBER:
72-109649

PRINTED IN THE UNITED STATES OF AMERICA

To my Mother
whose love of knowledge
and love of life have
continually made her
one of the younger
generation.

THE AUTHOR'S ACKNOWLEDGMENTS

The book now presented is the result of the accumulations of the author's academic experience in the Elizabethan field. It is not designed primarily for any special year or occasion, but its natural relation to the Shakespeare Ter-Centenary now being celebrated indicates this as the appropriate occasion for its publication.

My thanks are due to these authors and publishers who have courteously allowed me the use of illustrative or other material. I owe acknowledgments to Professor A. H. Thorndike and the Macmillan Company for permission to use, from *Facts about Shakespeare,* by A. H. Thorndike and W. A. Neilson, the chronological table of Shakespeare's plays; to Sir Sidney Lee, his American publishers, the Macmillans, and the English, Smith, Elder & Company, for the use of several illustrations, especially for the rare portrait of the Earl of Southampton, which is the property of the Duke of Portland. To M. Jusserand and his publishers, G. P. Putnam Sons and Fisher Unwin, my thanks are due for several illustrations from *The English Novel in the Time of Shakespeare.* M. Jusserand's permission is granted as "an indirect and more than modest contribution" to the Shakespeare Ter-Centenary. To Mr. Richard M. Saltonstall of Boston acknowledgments are made for the use of the portrait of his ancestor, Richard M. Saltonstall, in his robes of Lord Mayor of London in 1597, as it appears in the

THE AUTHOR'S ACKNOWLEDGMENTS

family book privately printed. Thanks are due also to Professor George P. Baker of Harvard University and his publishers, the Macmillan Company, for permission to reproduce the picture of St. Paul's Churchyard and several of the theatres from *The Development of Shakespeare as a Dramatist;* to Longmans, Green & Company for the use of pictures from Halliwell-Phillips' *Outlines of the Life of Shakespeare,* and from Gardiner's *Students' History of England;* to the Charles Merrill Company for a few illustrations from Anderson's *School History of England;* to J. M. Dent & Co., and E. P. Dutton & Co. for pictures from Ordish's *Shakespeare's London,* Dekker's *Belman of London* in the Temple edition, *An Elizabethan Virginal Book,* and *Shakespeare and Music,* by E. W. Naylor.

O. L. H.

PREFACE

The effort to present to the general reader a vivid picture of Shakespeare, as set against the background of his own age, has of course been made many times, with success. The present volume attempts this with especial reference to Shakespeare productions or Shakespeare celebrations, and brings to bear upon them as many as possible of the resources and safeguards provided by Shakespearian research. The emphasis thus converges strongly upon Shakespeare and his plays, although the book is meant to be helpful in the production of any Elizabethan play or any representation of Elizabethan life; and much of the material offered is as applicable in these directions as in the other.

The need for such aids has increased very rapidly in the past few years because of the growing realisation that Shakespeare wrote his plays to be acted; and that the interest derived from a play is doubled by acting in it or even from seeing it acted. If such revivals or pageants — whether Shakespearian or otherwise — are to be attempted, they ought to be given with understanding and reasonable accuracy. Moreover, Shakespeare's age was so full of colour and motion and artistic resources of every

sort that there is no æsthetic reason why such efforts
should ever be misleading in what they present.
What is actually true of that time is far more delightful for production than any inaccurate imaginings could be; for no other age in England was ever
so rich in all the elements which make successful
pageantry — music, song, dance, exuberance of
spirit, contrasts in social types, lavishness in dress
and ways of living, and everything that suggests
brilliance and variety of life.

Part I provides the foundations on which the understanding of the latter half of the book should
rest,— the account of Shakespeare's England, of his
life so far as we know it, and of the more important
facts about his works. It is indispensable to *Part
II,* unless the reader brings to it from other sources
much knowledge of the Elizabethan age. *Part II*
proposes plans for Shakespeare festivities, fitting
most of them into plans for one large pageant, but
making any feature detachable for representation
without the others, and allowing for the general plan
to be diminished to such proportions as are practicable for a given group. It is of course highly undesirable that pageants shall be uniform, and the
number of variations possible with Shakespeare and
his age is infinite. This second section of the book
describes settings, outdoors and in, plans for laying
out grounds, simple Elizabethan structures, costumes
etc. It re-produces the musical notation and words
for Shakespearian and other Elizabethan songs, gives

music and directions for Elizabethan dances, games of various sorts and other forms of amusement; illustrates at every point where this is practicable; and at the end adds a bibliography for fuller information on the subjects involved.

A book such as this may not covet the praise of being complete; for the facts upon which it must draw are at once too many and too few. Scholars have, in the last few decades, made enormous advances in their knowledge of Shakespeare's age and indeed of Shakespeare himself; and many volumes would be needed for setting down all the facts likely to be useful in a book such as this. On the other hand, there are gaps in our knowledge at many points. Add to this that some of the material in existence is not now available, and that the instinct for selection inevitably works differently in each one of us.

The word *pageant* as used in the book calls for some explanation, in view of a present tendency among American makers of pageants. A curiously contradictory sense of caution makes many seek to restrict the name *pageant* to spectacular festivities which celebrate the history of a particular locality and involve a local if not a national patriotism. Such celebrations are undoubtedly pageants, but neither the dictionary nor the history of the drama would sanction such a limitation upon the terms. Nor would either sanction any emphasis upon this historical and patriotic type of pageant as peculiarly

entitled to the name. The word first came into
prominence in England in the days of the old religious plays. At times it designated only the wagon
on which the actors in these plays performed their
parts and were moved about from street to street.
At other times it evidently meant only the words of
the play; and very frequently it included all that was
involved in the entire Corpus Christi celebration,—
the procession, the large group of plays presenting
successively the story of the Bible, the wagons equal
in numbers to the plays, the various sets of actors, the
stage equipments etc.

Nor does the Elizabethan use of the word give
any precedent for restricting it meaning to the sense
now favoured by many. Indeed the meaning had
by that time been extended to include masques, dialogues, triumphs, processions, etc., together or separately with any other form of entertainment involving spectacle and some element of acting. Julia in
Two Gentlemen of Verona speaks of the custom of
giving " pageants of delight " at Pentecost, and cites
as one of them a play in which Ariadne is shown as
passionate in her love for Theseus, Prospero in the
Tempest calls the masque of spirits summoned by
Ariel a *pageant;* and Othello describes a naval movement of the enemy as " a *pageant* [i. e. a pretence, a
piece of acting] to keep us in false gaze." Instances
of other variations might be multiplied. The usage
of the word in the present volume reverts most nearly
to the custom of applying it to the large Corpus

Christi celebration as a whole,— the difference being that here it is applied to a Shakespeare celebration. In this sense the variations of a Shakespeare pageant are countless. Music, dancing, and a procession without formal dramatic performances may be called a pageant, if the festival spirit expresses itself among a group in colour and motion; so may a simultaneous presentation of several plays of Shakespeare's if they are given in the same spirit, and especially if they are given outdoors, where the opportunity for space and spectacle are larger. There is, however, no thought of limiting the term to even so comprehensive a use as is followed in this book.

Indebtedness in a book such as this, both to Elizabethan documents and to the researches of modern scholars is naturally very great. The effort has been to make all due acknowledgment even for intermediate sources. Occasionally material has been available from more than one source and in such instances acknowledgments have been attempted only to the one actually used. Of more personal acknowledgments there are also several. I owe to Mr. Winthrop Ames, of the Little Theatre, New York City, encouragement in the decision to undertake the book; to Mrs. Otis Skinner much counsel and in certain sections of *Part II,* a practical collaboration. Many of her suggestions have been embodied in this second part, and all of it has felt her influence, although its faults are entirely my own. I am indebted to Miss Margaret Haskell, one of my students in the Drama in Bryn Mawr College, both for valuable assistance in collecting material and for helpful suggestions at various points. To Mrs. A. B. Mc-Mahan I owe here, as in every task of my pen, encouragement and help in a score of ways. Finally I offer grateful recollection to Mrs. Frederick W. Boatwright for help not to be clearly defined but of the sort which went far towards making the book possible.

O. L. H.

CONTENTS

PART I

SHAKESPEARE AND HIS ENGLAND

PART II

A GUIDE TO THE PAGEANT

CONTENTS

LIST OF ILLUSTRATIONS

ILLUSTRATIONS

ILLUSTRATIONS

ILLUSTRATIONS

ILLUSTRATIONS

ELIZABETHAN SONGS AND DANCES

PART I

Shakespeare and his England

SHAKESPEARE PLAYS
AND PAGEANTS

I

THE QUEEN'S REVELS

To a very significant degree Queen Elizabeth's passion for amusement paved the way for Shakespeare. When her reign began in 1558 there was hardly an English play deserving the name, except a few of the religious sort, and not one of the London theatres had come into existence. Many influences, of course, fostered the marvellous development of the drama in her reign, but she herself was the strongest outside force operating upon its life. She had been ruling six years when Shakespeare was born, and probably thirty or more when he began to write plays. During all that time her powerful and vitalising influence had been working directly upon theatres, dramatists and actors through the Revels at the court, and upon public sentiment by the fashions of dramatic entertainment which the court set up or favoured. That influence told in a thousand ways. Shakespeare's debt to the court as a patron of the drama was large at the outset of his career, and it grew with his growth. We can never fully understand either his dramatic inheritance or his development without visualising the dramatic activities of Elizabeth's court, and this we can do only by delving somewhat deeply into its records.

There is a ponderous collection of these records known as *The Documents relating to the Office of the Revels in the time of Queen Elizabeth,* and they belong mainly to the expense accounts of the royal treasury in Elizabeth's time; but along with the record of pounds, shillings, and pence goes an unconscious history of the surging activities needed to keep the Queen entertained, and of the intimate connection between court entertainments and the London theatrical life with which Shakespeare's work was so intimately bound up.

Seasons of Dramatic Entertainment at Court.

The special occasions for dramatic festivity at court were the holidays associated with religious seasons — Christmas, Candlemas, Shrovetide, Easter, and Whitsuntide, etc., the visits of distinguished guests — especially of royalty or the ambassadors of royalty — or weddings; other occasions, as well, developed, of course.

Types of Entertainment.

At the beginning of Elizabeth's reign court entertainment was an odd motley of acrobatic performances, fireworks, knightly exercises, æsthetic spectacle, and extremely simple beginnings of the drama.   In a sense,

Elizabethan drama remained unformed to the end, although there was a steady improvement among the better dramatists in their grasp upon the essentials of dramatic technique. By the mass — and the number of Elizabethan dramatists seems almost countless — the subtler differentiations among types of drama were largely neglected; and an artistic conscience towards formal questions of technique was a rare possession. The descriptions, in the Revels documents, of the plays provided at court in the earlier years of Elizabeth's reign, show the intention to tell a good story, or to have a brilliant spectacle, or to do both, as the guiding impulses in what was somewhat indulgently called a play. John Lyly, the author of the court play *Endymion*, speaks for many of his contemporaries when he makes the speaker of the prologue say:

" We present neither comedie nor tragedie nor storie nor anie thing but that whosoever heareth may say this, ' Why, heere is a tale of the Man in the Moon.' "

The accounts of separate plays, as of " a pastime, a pastoral, a history, an invention or play," suggest a half-artless desire to amuse and be amused; and many of the titles themselves show the casual ways of the playwrights, and the dominance of the story interest: *A Pastorall or historie of a Greeke Maide, A Comedie called delighte, A storie of Pompey, A Comodie or Morrall devised on a Game of the Cards, A matter called Praetextus, An Invention called Fyve playes in one, An Inventyon or playe of the three Systers of Mantua, The Historye of the Knight in the Burning*

Rock, The History of Cipio African, Timoclea at the Sege of Thebes by Alexander, The Historie of the Solitarie Knight, etc.

This extreme simplicity of dramatic structure, so marked, even in most of the plays given by professional companies early in Elizabeth's reign, gradually gave way to much more complication of plot interest, if not of characterisation, in the plays presented by the better London companies. Even when these companies were playing at court, however, the plays representing their fullest development, the court was devising for itself entertainments in which the dramatic interest hung by a very slender thread, and it continued to devise them. Neither in Elizabeth's reign nor in that of James I is there any indication that lords and ladies cared to devote long hours to memorising or practising intricate parts, and the entertainments in which they themselves took part continued to show a minimum of dialogue and a maximum of spectacle, with plot and characterisation often negligible. Even allowing for this, however, there is a very evident desire to give a dramatic cast to as many of the court festivities as possible, and it is often amusing to see how slight is the claim to being drama, or even a story. Masques, pageants, and triumphs were the favourite devices for the nobility themselves — the Queen not being given to participation in them — and it is impossible to distinguish clearly among the three, although the masque called more definitely than the other three for music and dancing.

There is a record of a triumph which illustrates the prevailing fashions in court entertainment, being hardly more than a dramatic frame built around a tournament in honour of the Queen. A castle, or "Fortress of Perfect Beautie," was erected close to the palace as a token that Elizabeth herself was its keeper and prize; and certain courtiers, who represented the foster "Children of Desire," laid claim to it. Their declaration of war against the Queen unless she would surrender the fortress, was delivered to her by a costumed messenger, and she responded by naming a day when the challenge would be answered by the knights of her defence. When the court assembled on the appointed day, Sir Philip Sidney, Fulke Greville, the Earl of Arundel, and many other court notables were seen to be among the knights, some to attack the fortress and others to defend it. At a signal a boy in costume sang aloud this summons to the Queen: "Yeeld, yeeld, O yeeld, you that this fort doe hold," etc. Another boy sang to the foster Children of Desire; there was music; cannon scattering sweet odours were discharged; the knights attacking the fortress mounted upon scaling ladders; footmen threw flowers and other friendly missiles against the walls; the defendants appeared and the battle was on, lasting with intermissions until the next day, when the Children of Desire sent their humble submission to the Queen and confessed that they could never hope to capture the fortress. Various surprising personages took part in the occasion — Adam and Eve, an angel, etc. The

entertainment was devised in honour of French ambassadors at court, as was also another in which six
ladies played at tournament with six gentlemen who
surrendered to them. In still another the Duke d'Alençon, a suitor for Elizabeth's hand, was represented as
bound to a rock, but being drawn away from the rock
by two figures, Love and Fate, until he found himself
at Elizabeth's feet.

Another triumph participated in by the nobility
illustrates the impulse to make the old disputation or
debate more dramatic. It was devised by the Earl of
Essex in honour of the anniversary of the Queen's
coronation, and evidently gained him some prestige for
ingenuity, although it can hardly be called original.
Essex himself is the central figure and is encountered
by three people who try to persuade him, each in turn,
to their several ways of life. One is a hermit, who
presents him with a book of meditations; the second, a
secretary of state, offers him a volume of political dis-
courses; and the third, a soldier, tempts him with
"orations of brave battles." Each presses upon the
earl the special advantages of his calling; but to all
their arguments his squire makes answer for him that
the best calling of all is that of serving the Queen, his
mistress. Nothing shall ever tempt him from that.
Watchful listeners identified all the characters with
people known at court, and read much into the speeches
that were spoken, claiming that the device had been
used to convey too much. The record of the occasion
closes with this pessimistic note:

"The world made many untrue constructions of these
Speaches, comparing the Hermit and the Secretary to
two of the Lords, and the soldier to Sir Roger Williams.
But the Queen said that if she had thought there had
bene so much said of her, she would not have been there
that night; and soe went to bed."

The Office of the Revels.

The Queen's Revels were in charge of a part of the
royal establishment known as the Office of the Revels
— the name being applied somewhat loosely to the
officers, or the building, or to the organisation as a
whole. The Office had sprung from humble beginnings but was already by Elizabeth's time an elaborate
and influential part of the court life. It seems to have
had its earliest beginnings in a royal custom to appoint
for special occasions some ingenious and learned person who could devise the court entertainment sought.
Later on, the responsibility was placed in a more permanent way upon a sergeant of the household with
grooms and others to assist him. It happened, however, that King Henry VII sought for this work Sir
Thomas Cawarden who was a member of his Privy
Chamber, but was known for "his skill and delight
in matters of device." The knight "did mislyke to
be tearmed a sergeant, because of his better countenance
of roome and place; . . . and so became he, by
patent, the first Master of the Revels," with an honourable rank in the King's household and on all public
occasions. To aid him in his duties, three other of-

ficers were appointed : — a Clerk Comptroller, who was closest to him in authority; a Clerk, who kept the accounts; and the Yeoman, who was keeper of the wardrobe and probably had most of the direct contact with the large force of workmen employed by the Office. During nearly all of Elizabeth's reign and of Shakespeare's dramatic activity the Mastership of the Revels was held by Sir Edmund Tylney, who succeeded to the post in 1560 and held it until 1610.   All that is said here of the Office and its doings comes from its records when he was directing it.

Duties of the Office.

The general scope of its work may be suggested by this description which the Clerk prefixes to one of the reports of its expenditures :

" The Office of the Revells comprising all maskes, tryumphes, Plaies, and other shewes of Disporte, with Banquetting howses and like devises to be used for the Amusemente of the Queens Maiesties most roiall Court and her highness recreacion and pastyme."

The records show, too, this account of the abilities called into exercise in the management of the Office :

" The conninge of the office resteth in skill of device, in understanding of historyes, in judgment of comedies, tragedies and showes, in sight of perspective and architecture, some smacke of geometry and other things; wherefore the best help is to make a good choice of cunnynge artificers severally, accordinge to their best quality."

In more modern English, it was the duty of the Revels' Office to furnish the court with the best dra-

matic entertainment which England afforded, and to
supply the court with all necessaries when it was pleased
to entertain itself with masques, triumphs, etc. Besides this, it must be busy devising new forms of
court entertainment and must make and care for all
the costumes and properties needed for these or the
others.

The largest bulk of the activity of the Revels' Office
had to do with the professional companies from the
London theatres and elsewhere. They submitted their
plays to be tested by rehearsal and, if accepted, were
equipped by the Master with such costumes and properties as were needed, besides having their own performance altered in whatever way the Master saw fit.
The whole relation of the London players to the Revels,
and the powerful influence operating upon them from
it, comes to light in the expense accounts beginning at
Christmas in 1579 and lasting through Shrovetide of
the following year. There are charges for the players
coming to have their plays tested, for the hauling of
their costumes and properties to be used in the rehearsals; records of choosing ten plays out of many
presented for choice; and charges again for sundry
other rehearsals before the plays accepted were considered in proper form for the Queen to see them.
Following these are various entries, showing how
laboriously the Office strove to supply each of the companies with all the equipment needed for the best success, evidently examining with some care whatever
the actors themselves had provided, but in most in-

stances completely supplying the play at the expense of the court.

Authority of the Master of the Revels.

In the execution of his duty to provide the Queen with the best, the Master was armed by her, early in her reign, with the power to command the services of actors, playwrights, tradesmen, workmen, etc., whenever needed, and as long as needed; also, to punish with as long a term of imprisonment as he chose those who dared to disobey his summons.   His power to decide whether plays should be given at court soon led to his authority to grant or withdraw licences for all plays given outside the court, in London or elsewhere; and also to grant or withhold licences to travelling actors wishing to play outside of London.   Later on he was given the right to licence the printing of plays, as well as performances — the two rights being by no means identical, since an Elizabethan play was not usually printed by its owners as long as it was proving successful on the stage.   This right of licencing gave the Master power to order any alterations which he desired made in the plays and to withhold the right of performance until all had been made.   For the court performances such " reformations " might have to do with the artistic results he desired; in plays licenced for the public stage, they usually concerned allusions which he considered dangerous for religious or political reasons.   Once, when a hot religious quarrel, was raging in England, the Master ordered the closing of all the theatres in London, because the players could not be trusted, even on the stage, to let the quarrel alone. At another time when a play called *The Isle of Dogs* displeased him, he caused not only the closing of the theatre where it was being performed, but the imprisonment of the actors taking part. Sometimes he was called on by one company of actors to prevent another from stealing their play. This he could do by forbidding the dishonest company to perform it, and he exercised this authority once in behalf of one of Shakespeare's plays which the Red Bull Theatre had stolen for performance by its actors. There is a record of a fee paid the Master of the Revels by Shakespeare's company for forbidding the Red Bull actors to use the play.

In every way, then, the Office of the Revels, and especially the Master, had become, by the middle of Elizabeth's reign, a force to be reckoned with. It is hardly to be wondered at that Lyly, successful dramatist and novelist as he was, died a disappointed man because, after many years of waiting, he had failed to secure the Mastership for which he had yearned. The fees which were poured into the Master's hand in the exercise of all his powers for granting licences were enough to arouse envy, and his authority was a thing to be coveted by the ambitious. It lifted him into the position of a grand arbiter for the Queen in matters affecting all the dramatists, theatres, and actors of the time; and showed that the Queen meant not only to prove herself a patron of the drama, but to restrain it at any point where complete liberty seemed to her undesirable. She was willing to protect the drama from the enmity of the Puritans, and she did it a vast and continuous service in that: but she meant, through the Master, to protect the government, and religion, and even the Puritans, to a certain degree, from the drama; and she used her power vigorously in that direction too. She was equally wise in both policies.

The Building. *(See Fig. 24, Facing Page 55.)*

The building where the Office of the Revels was lodged bore the interesting but somewhat inappropriate name of St. John of Jerusalem. It was a part of the system of buildings connected with an old monastery which, like many others, had been broken up in the time of Henry VIII. The rooms assigned to the Revels' Office were evidently far too small and unworldly in their provisions and there are many complaints about them. There is a curious irony, too, in the fate which made the London monasteries foster in their own decay the revelries of both the court and the city. It was at St. John of Jerusalem that for many years most of the dramatic entertainments at court were made ready, and the theatres of Blackfriars and Whitefriars served the city as well as the court.

Workmen and Tradesmen Assisting the Office.

Perhaps nothing shows so vividly the Queen's interest in dramatic entertainment and her exacting standards for its presentation as the army of humbler

workers required to make ready for the plays given
before her.   Long as the list here cited is, it is probably very incomplete except for the given time and for
purely chargeable labours.   There are tailors, embroiderers, painters, mercers, property makers, haberdashers, porters, upholsterers, drapers, silkwomen, fur-
riers, chandlers, armourers, buskin-makers, hunters,
patternmakers, joiners, coffer-makers, wire-drawers,
messengers, silk-weavers, linen drapers, stationers,
feather makers, smiths, basket-makers, wagon-makers,
plasterers, " deckers of the house with birch and ivy,"
horseshoers, iron-mongers, etc.   There were " the
tutors to teach the children their parts . . . and jes-
tures meete," when the child actors were performing
before the Queen; the " musicians that towghte the
ladies "— probably court ladies taking part in a
masque; the " women that wayted tattyer [to attire]
the children " performing, and " an Italian woman
. . . to dresse theier heades "; the Italian, Petruchino
Vbaldmas, who was required to translate " certen
speaches into Italian to be used in the masque "; the
" musitians who played at the proofe " [i.e. the rehearsal before the Master of the Revels] of Dutton's
play; Benbow, who acted inside the monster; Robert
Baker, who was paid " for drawing of patternes for the
playe of fortune and altering the same," etc., etc.—
all intent upon amusing the Queen and her court.

Management of the Office.

As a business the Office was a marvel of bad management.   Nearly everybody involved, from the Queen's treasurer to the humblest tradesman, complained strongly over the condition of affairs; but there is little proof that any of the abuses were redressed.   From the Master to the Yeoman the officers, although keen for financial gain, seem to have enjoyed their tasks for the artistic pleasure involved, and their rambling fashions in business did not apply to their artistic results, or to all of their ways of achieving them.   Their eyes were fixed firmly upon success and they were merciless in their demands upon their humbler assistants in achieving it.   It was the underlings who felt the pressure most keenly: their hardships were often severe.   The same force was often required to work both night and day, and all must be ready at command to travel "with the workes" when the Queen went from one of her palaces to another, or to any other place in her realm where her own resources for entertainment might be required.   There was probably some glamour about being called to work for the Queen, especially about travelling out from London as a part of the royal retinue; but it is plain that the workmen often felt the pressure too heavy, and pursued their tasks with a grim or protesting reluctance. The protest comes out in such entries as this:

"Bryan Dodmer for Breade and Cheese . . . to serve the plasterers that wroughte all the nighte and might not be spared nor trusted to go abrode to supper."

But there were more serious hardships to the workmen and "purveyors" than even these; for there were frequently long delays before they were paid from the royal treasury, and it is evident that the Office itself felt keenly at times the disgrace attached to the long-deferred payments; for there is at least one very spirited protest to the higher powers. In *A Note of Things to be Redressed in the Revels,* attention is called to this disgrace, as well as to the losses of the Office and of the workmen, who in their distress must borrow on the court promises at a loss of fifty per cent.

"More there ys two whole yeares charges behinde un payde, to the greate hinderaunce of the poor Artyfycers that worcke there. Insomuche that there be A great part of them that have byn dryven to sell there bills or debentars [i.e. bills against the Queen] for halfe that is deve [due] unto them by the same.

"More yt hath broughte the offyce in suche dyscredet with those that dyd delyuer wares unto the offyce that theye will delyuer it in for A thirde part more than it is woorthe, or else we can get no credit of them for the same, which thing is A very great hinderaunce to the Queenes maiestie and A greate discredet to those that be officers in that place, which thinge for my part I Ame very sorry to see."

Then follows a petition of the creditors themselves:

"To our moste gracious sovereaigne Lady the Queenes most excellent Maiestye.

"In most humble wyse, The poore Creaditoures and Artyffycers which serve th office of your Maiesties Revells: are dryven of necessitye, thus now to trouble your Maiestie (more then otherwyse they wolde) by meanes of many evells which theye sustayne: through want of mony Due unto them in the saide offyce. . . . Wherefore, onlesse it maye please your Maiestie the sooner to graunt payment it cannot be but

that the myseryes of many must needes be very daunger-
ously augmented, and soom utterly vndone, which they moste
needefully beseeche your maiestie for godes cause to prevent accordyng to your gracious compassion whose dayes
of godly peace and Ioye, they duly beseeche almighty god
in mercy long to encrese.

"Poore Bryan Dodmer a Creditour to saue the labour of
a great Number whose exclamation is lamentable."

"The poore creditours and Artificers which serve the
office of your maiesties Revells moste needefully desyer payment of Dettes unpaide ij yeares and more, As may appere
by the Awditours declaracions delivered to Mr. Secretary
Wallsingham."

The instructions for the conduct of the Office en-
join it upon the Master to be equally careful to avoid
extravagance and niggardliness.

"The seconde meane [i.e. here the *recommendation* to
moderation] is that the Maister of the Office be appointed
and chosen such as be neither gallant prodigall, nedye, nor
gredye; for if any of these, surely he will never be fullie
liable to this order [i.e. likely to succeed in his work], but
make waist sucke the Quene, or pynche the poor, or all
three."

There must have been much complaint over the
amount spent by the Office, however, in spite of this
well-balanced injunction; for a tone of over fervent
apology and explanation runs through all the Revels'
accounts, and the records of repeated alterations of
garments to serve different plays brings a smile at the
ingenuity of the designer, as well as at the zeal of
the Office to show its great thrift. These items are
typical.

" All the blewe and purple clothe of gold of this Maske
translated into VI. hungarian garments with long sleves,
and ageyne translated iiij of them into wemens kirtels
[skirts] of Dianas Nymphes and thother twoo to performe
the winges and collors of the patriarkes maske."

" The fforestockes [front portions] of the sleeves . . .
being often translated, transformed and disguised are so
foreworne and to moche [too much] knowen as now any
more not serviceable."

Sometimes, too, it is explained, as an additional reason why certain costumes are no longer available for
use, that they were taken away by the lords who wore
them in the masque; at other times, that they were
granted to the professional players as part of their
payment for the performance at court.

The crowded quarters for the Office were a constant
source of discontent and there are many references to
it in the documents submitted with the bills of the
Office.   Later on, the dampness of the storing places
seems to have added itself as another grievance, for
its effect upon the costumes so elaborately tended.
There is an amusing note of protest to the crown
against two specific grievances.

First, a " very greate long wall " has so far decayed that
the clothes-press, set against it, has fallen down, and the
Yeoman in charge of it is " fayne to laye the garments upon
the ground to the great hurt of the same, so as . . . it would
pity you to see such stuff so ill bestowed."

" Next there is no convenient Romes for the artificers to
work in, but that tailors, painters, proparative [property]
makers and carpenters are all fayne to worcke in one rome,
which is A very great hinderaunce one to Another which

thing nedes not, for theye are slacke enough of them selves."

The protest to the Queen against the Yeoman's lending out the garments used in court masques spares the Queen none of the realistic consequences of such injudicious loans. She must know that a garment "takythe more harme by ounce [once] werynge Into the cytye or contre where it ys often vsyd, than by many tymes werynge In the cowrt, by the grett presse of people and fowlnes bothe of the weye and wether and soyll of the wererer (who for the most part be of the meanest sort of mene) to the grett dyscredytt of the same aparell which afterwarde ys to be shewyde to yowr Honor, etc." One may read how in a single year at least twenty-one loans of equipment for masques were made to those outside the court.

Some of the entries of loans are quite suddenly intimate in the life which they suggest: as when we read of the tailor in Blackfriars, who hired the court costumes and properties of a masque for a performance at his wedding; or where a certain Mr. Edward Hynd did the same, carrying them away even farther for his marriage in Kent; or where the yellow cloth-of-gold gowns were rented by the Horse Head Tavern in Cheapside. There was evidently a very democratic policy in the mind of the Yeoman, so long as the money was paid; for the record of the loan to the tailor jostles that of one to the daughter of Lord Montague, and one to the Lord Mayor as well. In this single custom one can see how the court practice of present-

ing handsomely equipped masques not only stirred those
outside to emulation, but provided them, at comparatively small cost, with the elaborate equipment actually
used at court. The very practice of celebrating festive occasions, such as weddings, etc., by the performance of masques among people outside the court,
was an imitation of the custom there; and so in a very
direct way both the habit and the equipment of masques
passed from the court to the people.

Concerning the unending line of those who came and
went for the Queen's diversion, there are also many
human details, lying along the path of the Clerk's
record of the expenses of the Office. Some of them
flash the life and its stress upon us with a vividness
that is almost painful; as where some cost is recorded
for " the children [child actors] who wayted all night
to see whether the Queen would have the masque or
no "; or where a payment to Mother Sparrow, who
cared for the children when they went back to London tired and hungry and cold, was set down; or where
a fee is named for the porter who " watched all nighte
at the blackffryers brydge for the coming of the
[actors'] stuf from the Coarte." Other imaginings
distinctly cheerful gather around that " Benbow who
plaied in the monster," a wonderful property devised
in the Office and moved around by Benbow as he in-
habited it in the play; John Kelsey who, merely " for
using his Dröme [drum] in the Duttons' plaie," received two shillings and seven pence — no mean sum
when the purchasing power of money was approxi-

mately eight times that of the present day; about the public players, too, who took away, as a part of their wages, some of the crimson damask garments belonging to the court; and the six ladies all " prepared and brought thither in Redynesses " to personate six chosen Vertues in a masque, but denied an appearance because of the " Tediousnesse of the playe " just ahead of their offering.

One further example of the Queen's voracious demand for dramatic entertainment at court may be cited. The prevalence of the plague in London prevented the professional players from giving their usual Christmas performances at court, and the Queen, not to be daunted by this fact, sent to Cambridge a peremptory request that a play written in English be made ready for presentation before her. The letter here given is the reply of the head of the university, well known in the history of Elizabethan drama. The consternation of its writer will seem justifiable enough in view of the shortness of the time available.

" Right Honourable: Our most humble duties remembered. Upon Saturday last, being the second of December, we received . . . [advices] from her Vicechamberlain by a Messenger sent purposely, wherein, by reason that her Majesties owne servants in this time of infection may not disport her Highnes with their wonted and ordinary pastimes, his Honour hath moved our University (as he writeth that he hath also done the other of Oxford) to prepare a Comedie in Englishe to be acted before her Highnes by some of our Students in this time of Christmas . . . Englishe Comedies, for that we never used any, wee presentlie have none: to make or translate one in such shortnes of time we shall not be able: and therefore if wee must needes undertake the business and that with conveniencie it may be graunted, these two things we would gladly desire: some further limitation of time for due preparation, and liberty to play in Latin . . .

"JOHN STILL."

Costume.

Much might be written of the splendour of the costumes for the court drama.   The Queen's own passion for dress was proverbial: the Master and his assistants in selecting and devising the costumes must have had a genuine delight in rich textures, brilliant colours, and lavish adornments of the highest sort.   There is nowhere in the description of the costumes a suggestion of the tawdriness or cheap imitation which we are apt to associate with stage finery.   Everything is done on a scale of unstinted elegance, frequently of magnificence almost regal in itself.   Cloth of gold and of silver, gold and silver fringes, and countless other suggestions of splendour crowd one another in the records of purchases.   There is a note of a hurried demand that went with the Queen's warrant to a Westminster shopkeeper for cloth of gold and cloth of silver; and the prevalence of these lustrous textures in Revels' accounts and the hasty methods of the management suggest many such peremptory journeys.   It is a luxury to the sense of colour and often to that of touch as well, to read the descriptions of many of the costumes. "Jerkins [i.e. close fitting jackets] of purple cloth of gold barred over [striped or possibly checked] with guards of green silver "; " long sleeves paned [i.e. striped with goods of another sort] of red satten and gardes [i.e. bands] of clothe of gold embroidered upon Orrenge colored Satten, the collers turned down with Orenge colour clothe of silver "; " karnacion clothe of silver with workes " [embroidered figures] ; " crimson sarcenett [i.e. fine soft silk] branchte all over," etc. All these may not be clear to us in each single word, but each description brings before us the sheen and splendour of courtly costume and an impression of rich colours chosen with art.

It is evident, too, from the records that nothing was considered too troublesome to be attempted in the designing and elaboration of costumes. Patterns were worked out with the greatest care and there are various notes of expenses for sending the patterns to court for approval. On one occasion the Master himself for two successive days went to consult the Lord Chamberlain about a matter of patterns, as the charge for his boat hire across the Thames testifies; and a further item shows that a hamper of Revels' stuff went also for the Lord Chamberlain to pass upon it.

It is not surprising that such careful and expensive standards for costume should have made what most of the professional actors brought with them seem inadequate or unfit, although costuming on the public Elizabethan stage was by no means to be despised as to richness. It is not surprising either that the players were sometimes glad to include in their compensation some

of the Revels' costumes they had used in the court performances.

Properties.

The properties evidently matched the costumes in
elaborateness and expensiveness, although the former
on the public stage seem to have been much more simple. Possibly the classical stage setting of two or
more houses, or the Italian elaboration of this setting,
had taught the English court the fashion of a much-
built up stage; but in any case it was given to houses,
battlements, mounts, rocks architecturally devised,
etc.; and it is clear that the " smack of geometrie " required of the Master, and the skill of carpenters,
painters, joiners, etc., were not left to lie idle in
the preparations for a play.   When *The King of Scots*
was played there were " divers howses . . . as Senators howses, Lobbyns howse, Orestines howse, Rome,
the pallace of prosperitie, Scotland, and a gret Castell
on the other side."   For another play, a mount, a
dragon with fireworks, a castle with falling sides, a
tree with shields, a hermitage, and a chariot were
among the properties.   There are charges listed, too,
for building " cities " and " towns " on the stage; one
for " a great citie, a wood and a castle "; various ones
for forests; and for one play, a chariot four feet long
and eight feet wide, with a rock upon it, and a fountain,
near by, fitly decorated to serve as the abode of Apollo
and the Nine Muses.   Thus, even in Elizabeth's reign,
the court kept its sumptuous scale of stage architec-

ture; and the spectacles achieved when the high vogue of the court masque came in with the reign of James I, almost exceeded the grasp of our overfed imaginations of to-day — their elaboration and intricacy were so great.

Of the rivalries among the many companies in suing for the royal hearing, even the Clerk has left no tale in his records, though we may well imagine they were no less bitter than those which raged among these same companies out among the plainer people of London. On the whole, however, the Queen's patronage of London actors was catholic and justly distributed. There was some hint of creating an aristocracy among actors when she chose out certain ones to be known as the " Queen's Players " or the " Queen's Company " and gave them the insignia of her favour; but in practice she welcomed all who were adequate for her entertainment, and the records of the Revels' Office show how ready the Master was to examine the products of all reputable companies, and what a large proportion of the London companies did actually perform before the Queen — thoroughly professional adult companies and companies of child actors, school children sometimes, none too well underway in the histrionic art, and many others with nothing to recommend them unless it might be the merit of their play.

II

THE QUEEN'S PROGRESSES

THERE can hardly have been a more devoted or in-
veterate visitor than Queen Elizabeth among all the
sovereigns of history, although she never travelled beyond the bounds of her own realm. She was prompted
in her goings largely by her interest in her people and
her wish to know her realm; partly too by love of adventure, and partly — so the uncharitable have whis-
pered — by a desire to shift to a few of her subjects
for a time the high cost of maintaining the royal household.

She is said to have visited about three hundred cities
and castles during her reign, and wherever she went
the tide of homage flowed around her. She travelled
in sumptuous state, with a vast retinue of her own and
such additional escort as chose to do her honour.[1]
A progress usually included visits both to towns and to
the country seats of the nobility, and besides the opportunity for the simple country people to see her
along the way, it was one of the pleasant features of
her progresses that they were often allowed to join

[1] It is said, too, that three hundred carts loaded with baggage
usually followed in her train, some of them so heavy as to be
drawn by five or six horses.

with the aristocracy of the castle in enjoying her visits and in contributing to her entertainment.   Moreover, the Queen, although grasping enough among those more nearly her peers, knew how to be gracious for any service, however crude, from her humbler subjects, and accepted what they offered for the spirit in which it was given.   On the other hand, her natural love of spectacle and magnificence made the nobility know that the most elaborate entertaining by them would please her best; and more than one of them was impoverished for life by his extravagant expenditures when the Queen came to visit him.   That she often used the royal prerogative, too, of choosing her hosts for herself is shown in such letters as the following, written in 1591 by Lord Hunsdon, the Lord Chamberlain, to Sir William More:

"I have thought good to let you understand that her Majesty is resolved to make a Progress this year as far as Portsmouth, and to begin the same the 22 or 23 of this month and to come to your house. She is very desirous to go to Petworth and Cowdry, if it be possible. . . . But I have thought good to let you understand that though she cannot pass by Cowdry and Petworth, yet she will assuredly come to your house . . . and so I commit you to God. In haste July 10, 1591, your very loving frend Hunnesdon."

One of the most elaborate of all the hospitalities provided for Elizabeth was that of the Earl of Hertford, whose small country seat, Elvetham, was chosen by the Queen as a stopping place in much the same way as when she was pleased to visit Sir William More.   The

2. THE CORONATION PROCESSION OF EDWARD VI PASSING THE
CROSS OF EAST CHEAP.

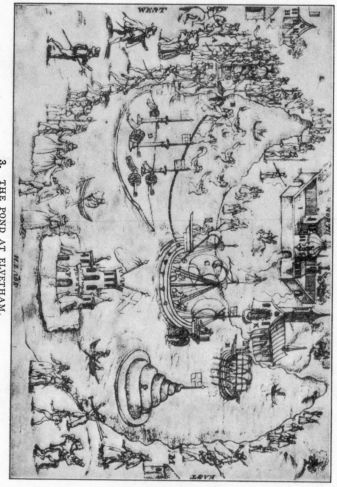

3. THE POND AT ELVETHAM.

Earl, hearing of her decision to visit him at Elvetham,
although he had much more ample residences elsewhere, set three hundred workmen to enlarging the
place sufficiently to accommodate the great throng to
arrive with the Queen.   Two hundred and eighty new
rooms were built for those attendant upon the progress, but not of the Queen's household.   " A roome
of estate " [state] with a withdrawing place near the
end for the Queen, was provided for the indoor amusements of the guests; separate "bowers," were arranged for the various groups — as for the Queen's
guard, her gentlemen-in-waiting, her " footmen and
their friends," etc.   Tables twenty-three feet long
were furnished for most of the bowers, and a system
of buildings was erected to be used in common for
feeding the host — among them a " pitchery," where
wines and ales were kept; a " pastery " where pastry,
one of the chief culinary delights of the court, was
made; a boiling house, a scullery house, a kitchen with
four ranges, kitchen for all comers, etc.

The centre of entertainment for the guests was a
pond made for the occasion in the shape of a half moon.
Its size is suggested by the three landing places within
its outer bounds — an island 100 feet long, a mount
40 feet broad, and a fort 20 feet square.   The music
was very subtly contrived and furnished in great
variety upon the water where there were many boats
gaily decorated.   Many of the sea gods, Oceanus, Neptune, Proteus, etc.— altogether " a pompous array of
sea persons "— performed their parts in the water,

gloriously dressed, and moving about breast high in
their rich costume.   One can well believe that the Earl
of Hertford felt for many a day the pinch of his
lavish entertainment to the Queen.

Amusements for the Queen on Her Progresses.

The amusements furnished the Queen on her
progresses were much like those of the court in their
emphasis on spectacle and simple dramatic devices; but
those presented by the country people were naturally
less sophisticated than the diversions of the court.   The
description which Armado gives in *Love's Labour's
Lost* of appropriate entertainment for the Princess of
France on a visit —" some delightful ostentation, or
show, or pageant, or antique, or firework "—might
pass as the standard for Elizabeth's entertainers as
well.   At Greenwich the villagers on one occasion provided for her diversion a challenge [in the nature of a
tilt or tourney], a masque, fireworks, and shooting.
The school master of the neighbourhood or one from a
distance was usually summoned, as in *Love's Labour's
Lost,* to combine the resources of his learning with
those of the castle and countryside.   When the Queen
was to visit Norwich the schoolmaster was called there
three weeks before her arrival and worked busily con-
triving devices of various sorts, most of them artless
enough, and some of them badly cumbered with learning, but all full of colour and life, as well as of loyalty.

The same tendency existing at court, to give all

possible amusements some sort of dramatic frame is
apparent here. The old-fashioned and academic disputation was giving way in the country, as at the court,
to dialogues with action and costume; formal orations
of welcome, formerly spoken by people of some importance in themselves, were more and more displaced by
costumed figures speaking as mythological characters,
or such symbolic characters as Fame, Desire, Peace,
etc. Sentiment, however natural, was dressed in devices which were usually thought out by some person of
learning; and costume, symbolism, and action gave
constant suggestion of dramatic intention, however
slight the hold upon plot interest or characterisation.

In very many of the amusements provided there
was recognition of the country setting and outdoor
life — a feature which in itself made many of the entertainments different from those provided by the
Revels' Office. Plays, or dramatic devices, with a natural outdoor background, such as the *Faery Queen,
The Ladie of the May, Robin Hood,* etc., were a part
of the customary recreation of the country people, and
needed only to be heightened into worthiness of presentation before royalty. Many versions of these plays
were set down especially for the coming of the Queen,
and others were entirely re-written for the occasion,
but their roots were in the customs of the country
people, and they spoke to the Queen of the life of her
subjects as well as of their homage to her. They
were often so incidentally presented in their outdoor
setting as to make the Queen think at first that she was

happening upon an actual event, and find herself bearing a necessary part in the entertainment.

The Ladie of the May, Sir Philip Sidney's dramatic interlude which was played for the Queen on her visit to Leicester's seat, Wanstead, in 1578, shows the way in which the life of the people and the Queen herself were brought into a simple outdoor play. It suggests, too, the rôle of the schoolmaster in the eyes of many villagers, and the dramatic form which a disputation could assume. This time the nucleus of the debate is the question as to whether the life of a huntsman or that of a shepherd is more to be desired; but the dramatic frame about it almost obscures the idea of a debate and May day sports are gracefully woven in. The Queen's own unintentional part in the play comes out clearly in this account of it:

"Her Most Excellent Majestie walking in Wanstead Garden, as she passed down into the Grove, there came suddenly among the train one apparelled like an honest man's wife of the Country; where, crying out for justice, and desiring all the Lords and Gentlemen to speak a good word for her, she was brought to the Presence of her Majestie, to whom upon her knees she offered a supplication and used this speech."

Then follows the story of how an only daughter was beset by the loves of a forester and a shepherd, and of how, not knowing how to decide between them, she must submit to a bloody controversy for her hand, unless the Queen's presence can restrain them. She begged the Queen's help and disappeared. As soon as

4. QUEEN ELIZABETH AT TILBURY.

Likeness of Elizabeth not authentic, but picture suggestive for
pageant purposes.

5. QUEEN ELIZABETH GOING IN PROCESSION TO ST. PAUL'S, TO RETURN THANKS FOR THE DEFEAT OF THE SPANISH ARMADA.

she was gone, ". . . there was heard in the wood a confused nois and forthwith there came out six shepherds, with as many foresters, hailing and pulling to whether side they should draw the Ladie of the May, who seemed to incline neither to the one nor to the other side. Among them was Master Rombus, a schoolmaster of a village thereby, who being fully persuaded of his own learned wisdom, came thither with his autoritie to part their fray; where, for answer, he received many unlearned blows. But the Queen coming to the place where shee was seeing them, though they knew not her estate, yet something there was which made them startle aside and gaze upon her; till old father Lalus stepped forth (one of the substantiallest shepherds) and making a leg or two, said these words:

May it please your dignitie to give a little superfluous intelligence to that, which, with the opening of my mouth, my tongue and teeth shall deliver unto you, as it is, right worshipful audience, that a certain shee creature, which we shepherds call a woman, of a countenance, but (by my white Lamb) not three quarters so beauteous as yourself, hath disannulled the brains of two of our beatioust young men etc.

After him follows the pedantic schoolmaster, Rombus, who is interrupted in his Latin quotations by the May Lady, the cause of all the dispute. She sets both her lovers to singing for the Queen; a quarrel arises as to which has sung better; then a debate as to whether the forester's life or the shepherd's is better. The Queen, being of course the judge, gives the victory to the shepherd's life, and so gives the bride to the shepherd lover. Then all foresters and shepherds sing, the May Lady does homage to the Queen, and all depart.

Kenilworth.

We know best the festivities with which the Earl of Leicester honoured the Queen's visit to Kenilworth in 1575. Their magnificence brought them great admiration in their own day, and the interest in them was heightened by Leicester's ardent love-making to Elizabeth and by his wife's unhappy end.

On the way to Kenilworth the Queen feasted last at Long Islington, some miles away; then took her "pleasant pastime" in hunting while the rest of the journey was being accomplished. She reached Kenilworth about eight o'clock in the evening and at every turn a welcome and a spectacle were waiting for her. There was a sybil in white silk at one gate; and a very large and stern porter also in silk at another, claiming to resent all the noise of the arrival until he discovered that Elizabeth was the guest, and then surrendering all his authority. Trumpeters on the walls blew their welcome from silver trumpets five feet long as the Queen passed through the second gate, and the Lady of the Lake, attended by nymphs, floated towards her on the water, speaking a welcome; while the island, set inside the water, was ablaze with torches. Then the Queen passed over a wonderful bridge whose seven posts on each side were decorated with symbolic offerings. At the end of the bridge stood a poet dressed in "a long ceruleous garment," with wide sleeves of blue and under those others of crimson. He told all the meaning of the offerings on the bridge and added his welcome. Finally, with the pealing of guns and the noise and flare of fireworks, the Queen entered the inner court and her welcome was accomplished. During the twelve days of her stay there was more hunting, much music, a fight betweeen bears and bandogs, an Italian " doing feats of agility," a combat of English and Danish knights, a mock marriage, a masque, a show on the water where Arion appears on a dolphin's back and sings to the music issuing from the dolphin himself, the Hock Tuesday play by the actors from Coventry, etc. There was also a more formal play " two hours long," although the historian was not interested to set down its name; and, incidentally for our purposes, there was a banquet at which three hundred dishes were served.

On the whole it cannot be said that the Queen's progresses added much of high dramatic value to the great results which were being achieved in London, although they played a significant part in the development of the drama. This was natural enough. Most of the entertainments given were devised largely as expressions of homage and welcome, and as the framework of beautiful outdoor spectacle. They were given, too, in most instances, by amateurs, frequently by crude ones, in recognition of the Queen's pleasure in such festivities; and they had a reflex influence upon those who gave them, because the stimulus of a royal audience stirred many a rustic group to do its best, and thus furnished them with the same incentive which was spurring the London actors and dramatists on to their triumphs. They rounded out, too, the Queen's contact with all phases of the dramatic activity of her realm, and increased her understanding of the artistic standards and recreations of city, village, country and castle, and of all the social orders.

It ought now to be clear that the Queen's interest in drama and dramatic spectacle was an energising fact at almost every point in the recreational life of her day. The very protection which it brought to plays and actors at a time when the Puritans were unceasing in their attacks and when the brand was still heavy upon the actor's calling, involved an immeasurable advantage to the arts of the drama. That, in itself, helped to bring intelligent legislation, by which the self-respecting actor could be distinguished from a lawless stroller and receive the legal support of a member of the nobility. It did even more, however, in furnishing London actors and playwrights a generous court patronage and a standard which introduced a healthy spirit of competition. It heightened among the people the spirit of loyalty to the Queen and that of community of interest with her, making her in a sense the centre of their dramatic inspirations and of their love for the drama. It tended to make her the theme of many plays, and to multiply the number of dramatists, theatres, and actors. It established con-

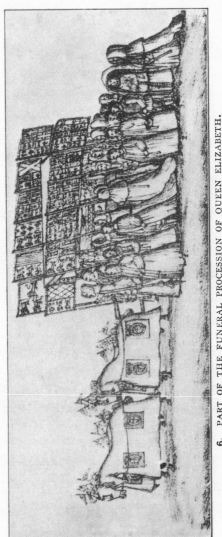

6. PART OF THE FUNERAL PROCESSION OF QUEEN ELIZABETH.

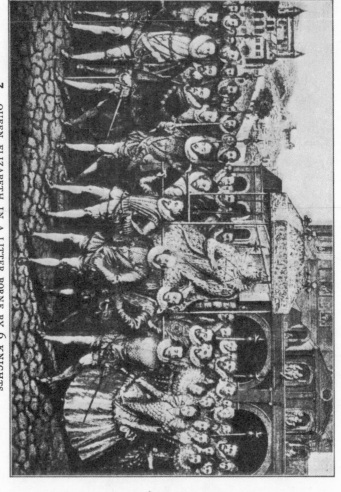

7. QUEEN ELIZABETH IN A LITTER BORNE BY 6 KNIGHTS.

At the Marriage of Lord Herbert and Miss Anne Russell, Blackfriars, June 16, 1600.

stant contact between the court and public theatres,
gave the Queen the opportunity to see what her people
were achieving in dramatic art, and public actors the
chance to present their plays with an entirely adequate
staging.   It is no mere accident of chronology that the
drama of her day is called the Elizabethan, nor is it any
wonder that the name kept its hold upon all the drama
which followed until the closing of the theatres in
1642.

III

LONDON IN SHAKESPEARE'S TIME

THE QUEEN

The Spirit of the Age.

PAUL HENTZNER, a German traveller in England, who saw Queen Elizabeth when she was already old, has left this description of her:

"Next came the Queen . . . very majestic; her face oblong, fair but wrinkled: her eyes small, yet black and pleasant . . . her nose a little hooked; her lips narrow . . . she had in her ears two pearls with very rich drops; she wore false hair and that red; upon her head she had a small crown reported to be made of the gold of the celebrated Lunebourg table. Her bosom was uncovered, as all the English ladies have it till they marry; and she had on a necklace of exceeding fine jewels; her hands were small, her fingers long, and her stature neither tall or low; her air was stately, her manner of speaking mild and obliging. As she went along she spoke very graciously, first to one, then to another, whether foreign ministers or those who attended for different reasons, in English, French, and Italian; for besides being well skilled in Greek, Latin, and the languages I have mentioned, she is mistress of Spanish, Scotch, and Dutch. . . . In the Antechapel near the hall where we were, petitions were presented to her, and she received them most graciously, which occasioned the acclamations of 'Long Live Queen Elizabeth.' She answered it with, 'I thank you, my good people.'"

8. QUEEN ELIZABETH.

Queen Elizabeth.
The Original by Isaac Oliver, late in the Collection of J. Most

Her Autograph from an original Letter in the Possession of
John Thane.

9. QUEEN ELIZABETH AND HER SIGNATURE.

A queen by nature, in her consciousness of power and her belief in her right to power, Elizabeth was of course an endlessly interesting study in the contradictions of her character. It is a commonplace to tell how she combined statesmanship and coquetry, love of learning and erudition of her own with exaggerated feminine vanities; selfishness in trifles with a certain profound self-abnegation for her people, extravagance with niggardliness, etc. Her passion for worldly enjoyments and material splendour was in strange contrast to her parsimony in gifts, and it was said of her truly that she was " never profuse in the delivering out of her treasure, but paid many and most of her servants part in money and the rest with grace."

The earlier years of her reign were rendered anxious by religious dissensions and by the enmity of Mary, Queen of Scots; and whatever we may think of her power of compassion she showed her courage and energy of character — possibly her statesmanship as well, according to the ideals of the time — in the execution of a rival who would otherwise have proved a constantly disturbing influence in the realm. The Catholics among her subjects were, from the beginning, arrayed against her, both because of her father's establishment of the Church of England, and because of their partisanship for Queen Mary; but on the whole she was skilful in dealing with them, as with the Puritans, whom she never offended past forgiveness by her love of worldly pleasures. Probably no woman ever courted or received more personal adulation, and a large proportion of Elizabethan literature is concerned either primarily or incidentally with doing her honour. Her subjects, especially her courtiers, knew her susceptibility to compliments and furnished it unstintedly; but in a very real sense all the homage tendered her was genuine, for no other sovereign ever stirred the people's hearts with deeper loyalty or answered it with a sincerer devotion. Nor has any age given the Englishman more cause for national pride.

Countless conditions crowned the age as supreme. Then at last England became firmly united and at peace; and her power was increasingly felt abroad. The victory over the Spanish Armada raised patriotic pride to the highest pitch. English explorers were on all the seas — Frobisher on the coasts of Labrador and Greenland, Drake circumnavigating the globe, Sir Walter Raleigh founding Virginia, London merchants establishing the East India Company, the Bermudas being visited, etc. The national imagination, as that of the individual, was being quickened by the tales of voyages and new lands. Italy, France, and Spain were all pouring in influences for literature, for art, and for habits of dress and living; and at last the Renaissance was fully at work in England. Interest in the classics was widespread and often passionate. Seneca, Ovid, Plantus, and Virgil were far more familiar names than they had ever been before or seem likely to be again. A host of translators were busy making continental and classical literature available in English; and many of them were inspired by a patriotic desire to furnish England good models for literature and to help her take a higher place among the cultured nations of Europe. Literary criticism began to define itself in the effort to build up certain standards of taste and judgment; and although the standards came chiefly from France and Italy, there was a patriotic insistence, among the more thoughtful, upon adaptation of all their borrowings to the genius of the English people. The prevailing conception of education, while perhaps lacking in thoroughness, if judged by our modern standards, was a very liberal one, and included physical and artistic development, as well as the mental. The nation itself seemed infinitely teachable, and receptive to influences in all the arts of living. Treatises on the arts of ruling, singing, riding, dancing, hawking, navigation, etc., chiefly translated from the Italian and the French, multiplied by the scores, and the English were busy in measuring up to what they understood of the life of Paris and Italy. In every way the mood of the time was alert, positive, and constructive. Achievement in every phase of public activity ran high; the creative instinct was busy in every literary form; and versatility was almost inconceivably rife. Sir Walter Raleigh is typical of this last, in combining the pursuits of a model courtier and explorer, a poet and prose writer, an official in turbulent Ireland, etc. Everything seemed somehow possible because the spirit of the time was young and exuberant, rampant and at high pressure everywhere. Life was in hyperbole of fact as well as of phrase.

It was inevitable, of course, that an age characterised by such intense vitality should generate many excesses. The very etiquette of the time reflects this excess in its multiplication of forms of " complimental courtesy." Alongside of this ran a frank brutality of attitude which we find it impossible to grasp to-day. The Queen demanded endless etiquette and ceremony, and Italian books of courtesy supported her demands. Hentzner reports that whoever spoke to her, when he saw her once in palace, spoke on his knees, and he declared that wherever she turned her face as she went along, all the people of the court fell on their knees. A model " Letter Writer " of the time instructs the youth taking leave of a lady to say, " Adieu, fair lady, you cannot but be weary of so troublesome a guest;" and the lady to answer, " Sir, I am much honoured in your presence and though not high enough for your merit, yet your entertainment is full of love, so that I shall be no way weary but happy in your longer stay if I may deserve that favour." Titles to books promised everything in their contents; and the dedication of a book left no spot in the patron's character unpraised. Extravagance of phrase constantly ran into a certain picturesque absurdity with its figures of speech and general heightening of emphasis.

Restlessness was of course an easy consequence of the feeling that everything was possible. Lyly comments upon it in the prologue to his *Mother Bombie,*

" Gentlemen, so nice is the world that for apparel there is no fashion, for musick no instrument, for diet no delicate, for player no invention, but breedeth satiety before Noone and contempt before night."

" Come to the Taylor, he is gone to the Paynters, to learn howe more cunning may lurke in the fashion than can be expressed in the making. Aske the Musicians they will say their heads ake with devising notes beyond Eloa. Enquire at Ordinaries, there must be sallets for the Italian; pick-tooths for the Spaniard; pots for the German; porridge for the Englishman. At our exercises, souldiers call for Trag-edies, their object is blood; Courtiers for Commedies their subject is love; Countriemen for Pastoralles, Shepheards are their Saintes. Trafficke and travell hath woven the nature of all nations into ours, and make this land like Arras, full of devise, which was Broadecloth full of workmanshippe."

The imagination, too, was susceptible and easily in-flamed. In spite of much satirical thought in the air, witches, fairies, and ghosts seem to have been accepted unquestioningly by the masses, and some of the current

10. THE HIPPOPOTAMUS SEIZING ITS PREY.

ideas about animals make the Elizabethans seem pos-sessed of the simple credulity of children. Topsell's *Historie of foure footed beastes* (1607) and his *Ser-pents* (1608) from which a few illustrations are here chosen, show the absurd ideas current then as to many animals familiar in one way or another to-day to almost every child. The hippopotamus is accredited with the voice and mane of a horse, the rhinoceros with the body and neck of a horse; the blood of the elephant is so cold that it is used in the summer to cool the heat of dragons. The lamia is the strongest of all beasts and very wicked, having a back like a goat's,

11. THE LAMIA.

forelegs like a bear's, a face like a woman, and scales like a dragon's; and using many wicked snares to entrap and destroy man. Much of this absurd belief gathered together and presented by Topsell was of course due to ignorance; but the ignorance was of the credulous constructive sort which loved to believe in the strange and picturesque.

On the other hand, there has rarely been among civil-

ised nations of the West an age fuller of frank brutality.   The same country which sent such generous
aid to Holland in its struggle for religious liberty knew
how to be very intolerant to its own heretics, whipping
and sometimes burning them at the stake.   Life was
taken and given easily, and punishments were ruthless,
often for very slight offences.   Hentzner wrote in his
diary that most of the English nobility had their heads
cut off, meaning that it was by the Queen's command,
and although this was hardly true, her imperious sense
of justice made the traitor's head rotting on London
Bridge a familiar sight; and the Tower, with its
gloomy prison, cut many a career short, even when
death was not the penalty for disfavour.   The description which an attendant on the Kenilworth festivities
for the Queen has left of the cruelties of the bear-baiting shows the stout nerves of the Elizabethans for
relishing a spectacle of suffering.

" It was a sport very pleasant to see the bear with his pink
eyes leering after his enemies approach: the nimbleness and
waiting of the dog to take his advantages; and the force and
experience of the bear again to avoid his assaults; if he
were bitten in one place, how he would rush in another to
get free; that if he were taken once, then by what shift with
biting, with clawing, with roaring, with tossing and tumbling,
he would work and wind himself from them; and when he
was loose, to shake his ears twice or thrice, with the blood
and the slaver hanging about his physiognomy."

Whipping, standing in the stocks or the pillory,
branding with hot irons, beheading, even burning alive,

and casting the offender into a boiling cauldron, were
all accepted penalties of the day.   There is a record of
a priest who was hung for a petty theft, and of an
author whose ears were cut off for expressing opin-
ions which would be entirely safe to-day.   Criminals
rode in open carts to their hanging, amid jeering
crowds.   Jews were objects of common ridicule and
baiting; insanity was treated as humorous.   The
economic pressure was intense, rivalries for patronage
were fierce, and brawls and duelling frequent.   Every
man went armed and the martial standards of the time
made physical contest the solution of many difficulties.
Roguery of all kinds flourished, and there was never
an age more ingenious in rascality.   Far more than
now, men preyed upon one another; partly from the
pressure of need and numbers, partly from an impulse
toward adventure.   The fraternity of fraudulent beggars was a well-organised and interesting profession,
and there were many fine discriminations in their type
of imposture.   *Upright men* were beggars who sought
money on pretence of having been wounded in the
Netherlands while helping the Dutch; *pailliards* wore
old cloaks patched to the point of evoking sympathy;
fraters imitated the look of churchmen and carried
counterfeit licences to beg for some charitable institu-
tions; *dummerers* sought alms on the pretence that
they could not speak; *whipjacks* claimed to belong to
the nobility and to have suffered great losses.
Counterfeit cranks feigned epilepsy, using soap to make
themselves foam at the mouth, and falling about the

streets. *Rufflers* were bolder rogues who went armed with cudgels. *Anglers* first begged from house to house to spy out convenient places for thieving; then used hooks at the end of long rods to snatch out of the windows sheets, coverlets, etc., which had been located by their spying. These more hypocritical of the begging fraternity were known as *canters,* and they used a certain jargon, for which an incomplete dictionary still remains.[1] The stanza given here in the jargon and then translated, is an example of some of their poor rhymes.

CANTER'S PROSE

" Stowe you beene Cose; and cut benar whiddes and bring we to Rose vile, to nip a boung; so shall we have lowre for the bowsing ken, and when be beng back to the Dewese a vile, we will filch some Duddes off the Ruffinans, or mill the ken for a lagge of Dudes."

Translated thus:

" Hold your peace, good fellow, and speak better words, and go we to London to cut a purse. So shall we have money for the alehouse; and when we come back into the country we will filch some clothes from the hedges or rob the house for a buske [wash tub] of clothes.

The extravagant fashions of dress and living made the habit of debt inevitable to many, and there were, besides, many people of the less ambitious sort who were familiar with the experience of imprisonment for debt. The pathetic letters of more than one Elizabethan dramatist begging for advance money on their

[1] This dictionary is given in the Appendix, p. 310.

plays, to pay them out of prison or to prevent their confinement, show how hard life often pressed upon them, as one of such letters will suggest. It is written by Robert Daborne, to a theatrical manager, Philip Henslowe, who furnished one of the chief markets for Elizabethan plays, and concerns Daborne's play, *The Arraignment of London.*

" I sat up last night to past twelve to write out this sheet, and had not necessity inforct me to yᵉ common place bar [Court of Common Pleas] this morning to acknowledge a ffyriall [final] recovery I would this day have delivered in all. I have been heartover [hereto-fore] of ye receiving hand; ye shall now find return to yʳ contens and yᵗ speedily. I pray, Sir, let me have 40s. in earnest of ye Arreighment, and on Monday night I will meet ye at ye new play and conclude further, to ye content I doubt not, resting myself and whole indevors.

" Wholy at yr service,

18 June, 1613.   " Rob. Daborne."

It was somewhat early in Elizabeth's reign that the Puritan Northbrooke in his *Treatise against Dicing, Dancing, plays and interludes with other Idle Pastimes* exclaimed:

" What prodigious apparel, what indecent behavious, what boasting, bragging, quarrelling and jetting up and down, what quaffing, feasting, rioting, playing, dancing and dicing, with other like fellowship that is among them, it is a wonder to see."

Many years later, Thomas Dekker, who himself often felt the penalty of the debtor's laws, describes a young gallant dressed in doublet and hose, armed with gilt

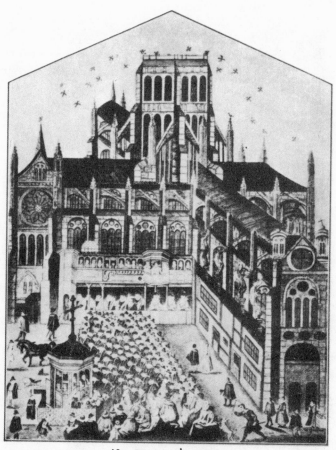

12. ST. PAUL'S CROSS.

13. THE BANKSIDE THEATRES AND LONDON BRIDGE.

rapier and poniard, and riding to the theatre " on a Galloway nag or Spanish jennet at a swift ambling pace," with a French lackey running before him with his cloak, and a " kennel of foul-mouthed sergeants " running behind him, threatening him for his debts.

London Itself.

In Shakespeare's time there were still some traces of the old wall which had shut in the small London of the past, and the seven gates — Oldgate, Bishopsgate, Moorgate, Cripplegate, Aldersgate, Newgate, and Ludgate — served to make neighbourhooods or precincts, in much the same fashion as the circuses Oxford, Piccadilly, etc., do in London to-day.   As the map here given shows, the old town had extended along the river in somewhat semi-circular outline from the Tower in one direction to the Blackfriars monastery in the other; but by Elizabeth's reign the population had pushed out beyond the gates for its residences as well as its pleasure grounds; and London may be said to have included, in its largest sense, not only much territory to the north but the river Thames and the part of the south side of the river, known as the Bankside. The Thames was, indeed, the great highway of the city and its environs, because of the bad condition of streets and roads, and it was the centre of a vast and varied life, with its hundreds of ferry boats plying north and south, east and west; its barges for the nobility and royalty; its merchantmen in from their trading journeys; and the explorers' craft standing at anchor.

A contemporary writer gives some suggestion of the possibilities of interest which the river afforded, in this allusion to the crowding of vessels there:

" A man would say, that seeth the shipping there, that it is as it were, a very wood of trees disbranched to make glades and let in light,— so shaded it is with masts and sails."

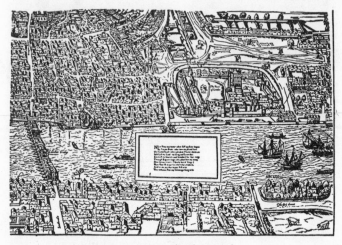

14.   LONDON (1560–1570).
The earlier part of Elizabeth's Reign.

And this entry in Hentzner's Diary fills out the picture:

" Upon taking the air down the river, the first thing that struck us was the ship of that noble Pirate, Sir Francis Drake, in which he is said to have surrounded this globe of earth."

A social life full of sturdy talk and tales of adventure must have surged along those wharves and among

15. THE BANKSIDE WITH THE EARLIER RINGS FOR BEAR-BAITING AND BULL-BAITING.

16. LONDON IN 1593, SHOWING THE THEATRES ON THE SOUTH
SIDE OF THE THAMES.

the vessels at rest; and it is said that the returned
mariners often earned an honest penny by serving as
watermen in the ferry boats.   There were many landing places with stairs along the river — some quite famous ones, as Paris Garden Stairs on the Bankside,
Paul's Wharf on the city side, Broken Wharf, the
Old Swan, etc. Blackfriars had also a well known
landing and was opposite Paris Garden Stairs. London
Bridge, as the picture shows,[2] was furnished with
houses on each side of it, although one of its twenty
arches had a drawbridge which permitted vessels to
pass through. The palaces of the nobility and of
the higher churchmen stretched along the river and
were reached by barges. Somerset House, Leicester
House, etc., were among them.

The pleasure grounds for London lay to the north
and to the south.   The first of these were on the city
side, near the place where the residence section ended,
and consisted of parks, animal rings, etc. Finnsbury
Fields was an important centre in this region. The
other grounds were in the part of London known as
the Bankside and were reached either by ferry or by
crossing London Bridge, and turning away from the
village of Southwark to the right. At the beginning
of Elizabeth's reign this region had consisted of open
fields, with an occasional place for bear-baiting or for
other crude forms of diversion. In time, however, a
succession of theatres began to appear there, some being used alternately for the animal baiting and others

[2] Fig. 13. Page 49.

being reserved entirely for dramatic performance. Ultimately the Bankside became much more popular than the northern pleasure grounds for entertainment of the more formal sort. Its popularity was a source of much income to the boatmen on the Thames, and the fashionable crossing was from the Blackfriars

17. THE STAR CHAMBER, WESTMINSTER.

landing on the one side to the Paris Garden Stairs on the other.

Within the city — using the word in its broader sense, not to include merely the part over which the Lord Mayor had jurisdiction — were Westminster Abbey and Westminster Hall, St. Paul's Cathedral,[3] the Royal Exchange, etc. Blackfriars was a district

[3] For other views of St. Paul's Cathedral see pp. 58 and 134, and p. 48 for Paul's Cross.

where various courtiers lived and where the chief private theatre was located.   In Cheapside was a row of goldsmiths' or jewellers' shops [4] and the Mermaid Tavern, so intimately associated with Elizabeth dramatists.   Eastcheap was the resort of butchers, tavernkeepers and cooks, and the Boar's Head Tavern, made famous by Falstaff in the Henry IV plays, was there.   In Bishopsgate at the Bull's Inn, Tarleton and others played before the first London theatre was built.   Newgate was already well known for its prison; Gray's Inn and Lincoln's Inn were the abodes of lawyers; the Charterhouse, later famous as a school, was then the home of the Earl of Suffolk; the churchyard of St. Paul's was much taken up with bookshops and book stalls, etc.

London had still many of the ways and surroundings of village life, with country fields close at hand, gardens attached to most of its houses, and barnyard animals somewhat too much in evidence.   The streets were narrow, unpaved, and unlighted, and this, with their open drainage, made it a point of wisdom for the cautious to keep to their homes at night — all the more because the darkness and the spirit of the times invited attack.   Constables and watchmen of various sorts meant to search out evildoers, went their rounds with torches as often as disinclination permitted, but they were notoriously inefficient and were the butt of much ridicule.   People went about on foot, in litters, or on

[4] A view of a part of Goldsmith's Row is to be found facing p. 28.

horseback in the early years of Elizabeth's reign, but seven years after her accession a Dutchman presented

THE BELMAN
OF LONDON.
Bringing to light the moſt notorious
villanies that are now practiſed
in the KINGDOME.
Profitable for Gentlemen, Lawyers, Merchants, Citizens, Farmers
Maſters of Houſholds, and all ſortes of ſeruants, to mauke,
and delightfull for all men to Reade,
Lege, Perlege, Relege.

Printed at London for NATHANIEL BVTTER. 1608.

18. TITLE-PAGE FROM THE FIRST EDITION OF
"THE BELMAN OF LONDON."

her with the first coach ever seen in England and this set a fashion of coaches which in time made the hired coach, or hackney, a serious rival of the ferry boats on

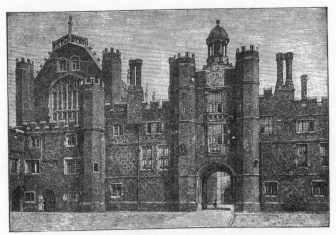

19. HAMPTON COURT PALACE.

20. GATEWAY OF LINCOLN'S INN.

21. GREENWICH PALACE.

Where Shakespeare acted before Queen Elizabeth in 1594.

22. THE THEATRE, 1576.

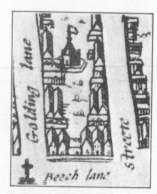

23. SECOND FORTUNE THEATRE.

24. ENTRANCE TO THE REVELS OFFICE.

South Gate of the Hospitallers of St. John of Jerusalem.

the Thames.   John Taylor, the water poet, complains loudly of this.

The London Corporation.

In order to understand important events occurring in Elizabeth's reign, one must realise that the city of London had a certain independence of the crown because of its own charter, and that it asserted this very tenaciously through its Lord Mayor, aldermen, etc., known together as the London corporation.   The legal limits of the city, within which the Lord Mayor had supreme jurisdiction, were carefully observed, and if a sovereign dared overstep these limits or any other civic rights, serious difficulties were likely to ensue. The palaces were all outside the city limits, Whitehall, Greenwich and Windsor being the chief ones, and the sovereign's entry into its bounds was always a matter of favour and welcome.   During all of Elizabeth's reign the Puritan element in the London Corporation was increasing in power and insisted on its right to restrain the diversions so loved by the Queen.   Some of her best diplomacy was spent in her dealings with those who could not understand why any arts which brought temptation in their train — as that of the drama did — should flourish at all.

One has only to read an account of the domestic establishment of the Lord Mayor and of his retinue on occasions of state to realise that he was no mean second in Londoners' eyes to royalty itself; and that the sceptre which he carried at such times was not a

meaningless symbol. Stow in his *Survey of London*
names "the days of attendance that the fellowships
[guilds of workingmen] doe give to the Mayor at his
going to Paules " [St. Paul's Cathedral] for worship.
These days were the religious holidays, Hallowe'en,
Christmas, New Year's Day, St. Stephen's Day, St.
John's Day, Twelfth Day, and Candlemas. On these
occasions large representations from all the workingmen's guilds attended the mayor, as did also the aldermen, dressed in scarlet gowns, the Chamberlain of
London, the Sergeants and Yeomen of the Chamber,
two Sergeant Carvers, four several Esquires, a sword
bearer, the Squire of the Common Hunt, the Common Crier, the Water Bailiff, etc.

The guilds of London, representing both merchants
and workmen of many kinds, and so both the middle
and lower classes, were in close organic relation to the
mayor and aldermen as a part of the corporation.
The same plan of organisation was followed in the
smaller towns throughout England, but the bond seems
to have been closer in London than elsewhere, both
among the members of a single guild, and between the
guilds and Corporation as a whole. Some of the
guilds represented in a feast for the Mayor in the
Guildhall in London were the grocers, mercers, drapers, fishmongers, goldsmiths, skinners, vinters, merchant tailors, ironmongers, haberdashers, salters, dyers,
leather-sellers, pewterers, cutlers, armourers, wax
chandlers, tallow chandlers, shearmen, cadlers, brewers, laundrymen or fullers, scriveners, butchers, bakers,

poulterers, stationers, embroiderers, bowmakers, arrow-makers, painters, masons, plumbers, stainers, carpenters, pouch makers, joiners, coopers, glaziers, tile makers, weavers, blacksmiths spur makers, wire-sellers, fruiterers, blade-smiths, etc.

Social Centres.

The taverns and ordinaries — corresponding to different types of our restaurants of to-day — were the

25. STAPLE INN, HOLBORN.

natural meeting places of a people given to much circulation and especially to much social life over the cup.

They were simple in structure and equipment, but at the ordinary one could feast heavily; and there, as well as at taverns, drink abounded. Inns are not always distinguishable from ordinaries and taverns, but were usually places for lodging as well as for food and drink. It would seem that a democratic spirit must have prevailed at such places, since all classes thronged to them;

26. ST. PAUL'S CATHEDRAL AND NEIGHBOURHOOD.
(The Upper Spire, burned with the rest of the spire and roof in 1561, was never restored.)

and the contact and conversation which such places naturally brought about offered excellent opportunity for observing the life of the time. Francis Beaumont's verses to Ben Jonson, as well as other evidence, show that the Mermaid Tavern was a popular haunt for the dramatists, and there is a seventeenth-century tradition that Shakespeare and Ben Jonson were the pitched champions of debate there, differing in their ways of persuasion as an English man-of-war would differ from a cumbrous Spanish galleon in a fight at sea.

Another favourite meeting place of the worldly minded was, somewhat curiously, a part of St. Paul's Cathedral, and its grounds or yard. The church, being apparently open all day, had gradually become a rendezvous for the least religious class as well as for the more devout; and in the nave, known as " Paul's Walk," were every day to be seen those who were fashionables and those who wished to be so esteemed, seeking out the newest features of costume, gossiping and mingling as would be done to-day in a club house or a fashionable hotel.   Business, too, of various sorts was transacted there by conference.

Paul's Churchyard, as the open space about St. Paul's was called, was not only a centre for the book trade, but a place for the favourite lotteries of many kind. Paul's Cross at the northeast corner was the pulpit from which preachers spoke on Sunday, usually with some special injunctions from royalty as to a policy to be furthered in matters of church or state.   It has much historical importance.

Houses and Furniture.

The houses of the period, even those of the wealthiest, were odd combinations of luxury and bad housekeeping, lacking many of our most common devices for cleanliness and convenience, but showing in their furnishings many marks of elegance.   Hentzner tells

us that in the country the houses were never more than
two stories high, but that in London they had usually

27.   EXAMPLES OF CARVING.

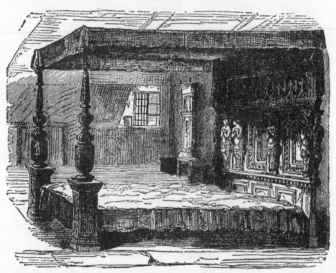

28.   BED IN HATHAWAYS' COTTAGE.

three and occasionally four stories.   He declares that
they were usually of wood except those which the

wealthy chose to make of brick; the wooden ones were frequently covered over with clay. Floors were left bare or strewn with rushes. It seems not to have been the custom to put many heavy pieces of furniture into a room, but certain articles, such as beds and chests, were made and chosen with great care, and very beautiful examples of them still remain. Many tables

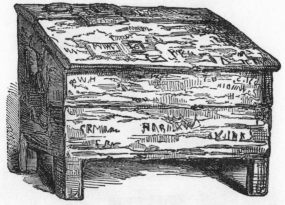

29. A DESK FROM THE STRATFORD GRAMMAR SCHOOL.
Called Shakespeare's, and Preserved in the Shakespeare
Museum.

also show fine workmanship. Hentzner testifies that even farmers had beds covered with tapestry, and the Elizabethan beds in the Hathaway cottage and Shakespeare's birthplace are handsome and imposing in appearance. The fact that Shakespeare saw fit to make his second best bed a special legacy is itself a proof of the esteem in which beds was held. Much of the furniture, however, was very simple. Much attention was evidently paid, too, to plate, and not only Shakespeare's will but those of other actors indicate that middle class people of means furnished themselves very lavishly with silver dishes and those of other metals, besides the smaller articles of silver. Fine glass was also much affected by the wealthy, and Harrison in his

30. OLD OAK SETTLE.
Called Shakespeare's Courting Chair.

Description of England tells us that many fortunes were made by London merchants importing Venetian glass to supply those who had grown weary of the fashion of silver vessels. Hentzner describes in his Diary " a most perfect looking glass ornamented with gold, pearl, silver, and velvet " which was estimated to have cost an enormous sum and was the property of a tailor.

Tables.

The tables of the prosperous middle class and no-bility were set with linen, glass, and silver chiefly, although the silver was mostly in the way of platters or trenchers, from which many could eat. Forks were a discovery of the Elizabethan period. Drinks were served in goblets or jugs of silver or Venetian glass, which are said to have been rarely set upon the table by the drinker, because what he left was given to one standing near his chair. In the house of a nobleman the throng of suitors for help and the strangers not of a rank to sit with him at his table is said to have been very large, and it was the custom after those of high degree had feasted, to send the food next to them, then to the serving men, and from them, to the poor, wait-ing in throngs at the gate. Hentzner gives a very full account of preparations which he saw executed for a dinner for the Queen, and although it must be borne in mind that no other feast in England would have been so ceremonious, a part of what he reports is suggestive of more general customs of the time. The dinner was at Greenwich Palace in the year 1598.

" A gentleman entered the room bearing a rod, and along with him was another bearing a tablecloth. After they had both kneeled three times with the ut-most veneration, the last spread this upon the table; and after kneeling humbly again, they both retired.

Then came two others, one with the rod again, the other with a salt cellar, a plate, and bread. When they had kneeled, as the others had done, and had placed what was brought upon the table, they too retired with the same ceremonies as those performed by the first two. At last came an unmarried lady (we were told she was a countess) and along with her a married one, bearing a tasting knife; the former was dressed in white silk, who, when she had prostrated herself three times in the most graceful manner, approached the table and rubbed the plates with bread and salt with as much awe as if the Queen had been present. When they had waited there a little while the Yeomen of the Guard entered bareheaded, clothed in scarlet, with a golden rose upon their backs, bringing in at each turn a course of twenty-four dishes, served in plate, most of it gilt; these dishes were received by a gentleman in the same order and they were brought and placed upon the table while the lady taster gave to each of the guard a mouthful to eat of the particular dish he had brought, for fear of poison. During the time that this guard, which consists of the tallest and stoutest men that can be found in all England, being carefully selected for this service, were bringing dinner, twelve trumpets and two kettle drums made the hall ring for half an hour together. At the end of all this ceremonial a number of unmarried ladies appeared, who with particular solemnity, lifted the meat off the table and conveyed it into the Queen's inner and more private chamber, where, after she had chosen for herself, the rest went to the ladies of the Court."

Foods.

The Englishman's appetite has always been primarily for meat and drink in the literal sense. An Elizabethan historian declares that " in numbers of dishes and changes of meat, the nobilitie of England . . . doe most exceed, sith there is no daie in manner that passeth over their heads wherein they have not onlie beefe, mutton, veale, lambe, kid, porke, conie, capon, pig, or so manie of these as the season yieldeth," but " some portion of the red fallow deer, besides great variety of fish and wild fowl, and thereto other delicacies." A dinner at a tavern is described as including " stewed mutton, goose, woodcock, capon, oysters, trout, salads, fruits and cheese." Hentzner notes the small amount of bread which the English eat in proportion to the meat consumed, and Harrison declares that, although merchants and gentlemen content themselves with from one to three kinds of meat when their tables are without guests, they ransack the country for " delicate meats " when their hospitality is to be tested. Another writer mentions a feast where a peacock pie was made with the fowl cooked whole, the head projecting through the crust. There is mention, too, of a boar's head served on a silver platter " with minstrelsy," a custom which was probably common enough in the Christmas season.

Workmen customarily lived " by such meat as the

butcher selleth "— beef, mutton, veal, lamb and pork, brawn and bacon, and supplemented these with fruit, cheese, butter, eggs, pies, etc. Potatoes, not being grown in England, were a luxury for banquets, and were brought from Spain, Portugal, and the Indies. Harrison tells us, somewhat puzzlingly, that most of the cooks for the nobility were " musical-headed Frenchmen and strangers."

Drinks.

There was much discrimination in wines and the wealthy were very ambitious to be known for their well-stocked cellars. Fifty-six kinds of small wine are known to have been in use, and some were brought from such distant points as Greece, Italy, Spain, the Canaries, etc. Ale and beer were the common drinks of the working man —" cakes and ale " being, of course, the synonym for the countryman's simpler feastmakings. Sack, or white wine well seasoned with sugar, was a favourite tavern drink; and romney, bastard, muscadel and malmsey, can only suggest the large variety of more expensive wines from which the wealthier Englishman might choose.

Sweets.

Harrison names as confections used by his Elizabethan contemporaries marchpanes [sweetened bread or paste] and tarts in many colours and shapes; conserves made from both foreign and home-grown fruits; jellies in the shapes of flowers, herbs, trees,

beasts, and fruits; suckets [sweet things to be sucked],
marmalades, sugar breads, gingerbread, and " sundrie
outlandish confections altogether seasoned with
sugar." The working out of intricate designs in
cakes and candies was evidently as important as the
taste of them, although the Elizabethans were much
given to eating sugar. One of the gifts presented to
Queen Elizabeth on a certain New Year's Day was a
marchpane made to form a miniature of St. Paul's
Cathedral with its steeple; and another, sent by the
Yeoman of the Queen's chamber, was in the form of
a tower " with men and sundry artillery in it."

The Use of Tobacco.

The introduction of tobacco, which resulted especially from the colonisation of Virginia, led to its adop-
tion to an extent fairly appalling to the few who ab-
stained. King James' *Counter blaste to Tobacco* declares that " some of the gentry of the land spend as
much as four hundred pounds a year " upon it; that
it has become a point of good fellowship in taverns,
homes, and elsewhere, and that any who refuse it are
held to be " peevish and no good company. Yea, the
mistress cannot in a more mannerly kinde entertaine
her servant than by giving him out of her faire hand
a pipe of tobacco."

IV

SHAKESPEARE'S LIFE

WHEN Shakespeare was born, Queen Elizabeth was
so new to the throne that England was hardly conscious of the glory destined to mark her reign. As he
grew through boyhood into young manhood in his
quiet country town, the brilliance and rich variety of
the age were steadily unfolding themselves; and in a
sense it might be said that he and the age came to
their maturity together. It was certainly not far
from the year of the Spanish Armada when he went
up to London to seek his fortune and, so, fell upon
playwriting.

Stratford.

In 1564, Stratford, the Warwickshire town where
Shakespeare was born, was possessed of about 2000
inhabitants. It was simple in its customs, and none
too cleanly or comfortable in its ways of living, but
self-respecting and law abiding as is the English fashion. In almost every phase of its life it was a typical
country town of its time — with many ale houses, a
very paternal town council, a grammar school to which
children were sent, at least for a time as a matter of
course; and a parish church which divided the honours

31. SHAKESPEARE: THE ELY HOUSE PORTRAIT.

32. SHAKESPEARE: THE CHANDOS PORTRAIT.
Attributed to Burbage. In the National Gallery, London.

of authority with the town council, and joined with it
to make attendance at divine services compulsory.
Bad as the means of travel were, the town evidently
felt some stimulus of contact with London, eighty miles
away; for there was much going up to London on
the part of Stratford youths and those of the country
around, to seek their fortunes. Records of appren-
ticeships to London printers from the time when
Shakespeare was sixteen years old until he was twenty-
nine, show a long succession of Warwickshire apprentices, many from Stratford itself. This one fact
would have built up, in so small a place, among the
youth of the town a certain sense of the nearness and
availability of London. Richard Field, later the master of the Company of London Stationers — a term
apt to include all we mean to-day by printers, publishers, and booksellers — was a Stratford youth, only
three years Shakespeare's senior. His rapid rise in
his calling must have made him seem to his Stratford
companions a shining example of what success in London might mean. Warwickshire men, too, of higher
birth, like Fulke Greville, later Lord Brooke, had gone
up to the court and become high favourites. The Earl
of Leicester, long the prime favourite at court among
so many rivals, had his country seat at Kenilworth,
only a few miles from Stratford, and gave the Queen
his famous hospitality there when Shakespeare was
still a child. Other Warwickshire men, like Henry
Neville, Edward Arden, or Edward Somers, must have
stirred Stratford interest many times and brought the

court very near by the misfortunes which crowded
upon them from royal disfavour.

There came along the highway, too, from London
strolling entertainers of many kinds, and other adven-
turers upon fortunes, whether actors, ballad-sellers,
rogues, puppet showmen or others — all a part of the
London life or full of reports of its doings. Not that
any of these glimpses of the outside world stirred
Stratford itself with an impulse towards progress; but
they inevitably widened the horizon of the young people of the town.

Stratford had, to be sure, a certain importance of
its own, being a market town, and a place for holding
semi-annual fairs, which brought in the people from
the neighbouring country and towns. The fairs were
the great gala occasions when the entertainers flocked
in with their plays, puppets, ballads, bears, etc.; and
when the outdoor sports of the season were at their
height. The town was not, however, lacking at any
time in recreations, as the difficulty which the town
council had in regulating them will testify. There
were bowling greens, archery butts, places for bull-
baiting and cock-fighting, all more or less characteristic diversions of the people. Besides, Coventry, only
a few miles away, was the centre for the great religious pageants and there is abundant proof in Shakespeare's plays that he somewhere gained a very vivid
intimacy with the sort of Bible plays performed in
Coventry and other small English towns. On the
whole, although Stratford may not have been superior

in any tangible way to most towns of its size, Shakespeare was fortunate in the place of his birth; for its wholesome love of diversion on the one side, and steady insistence upon law on the other, made for a normal development of its youth; and the contact with London was at least enough to be a call to ambition and a lure to the sense of adventure.

Shakespeare's Parents.

Of Shakespeare's mother we know comparatively little except that her family had some connection with the distinguished Arden family of Warwickshire, and that she brought her husband property through her inheritance from her father, a wealthy farmer of that region. We like to think that the poet inherited from her a certain intuitive understanding of the ways of gentle folk; but, whether this is true or not, she seems to have belonged to an obscure branch of the Arden family and to have had very little education, even making her mark upon legal documents instead of signing her name. She was the favourite daughter of the prosperous landowner, however, and must have grown up in some elegance there, as his will gives evidence in the list of furniture, etc. John Shakespeare, the poet's father, had been a tenant on her father's property, so the acquaintance between them had come about naturally enough. Her inheritance, at her father's death, of the Wilmcote home and fifty acres of land besides money, had the double value of emphasising her ancestral gentility and of giving her a substantial dowry; so that the match must have seemed a very good one indeed to her father's former tenant and to an interested neighbourhood. That John Shakespeare was fully alive to the suggestion of social prestige in his alliance is shown by his use of it later when he applied to the College of Heralds for a coat-of-arms. It should be noted also that the College of Heralds fully accepted this argument in granting the coat-of-arms, recognising the Ardens of Wilmcote as possessed of "ancient arms."

It is interesting, although perhaps precarious, to conjecture what temperamental inheritance the poet gained from his father. Shakespeare's biographers have perhaps not done justice either to the dignity or to the interest of his father's individuality, keeping their eyes fixed somewhat too insistently upon his tendency to become involved with the law — a tendency which he assuredly passed on to his son without marked diminution. It is disconcerting, too, that the earliest of the legal records concerning him shows him fined for not having removed a heap of refuse from before his door; but too much should not be made of this, for the standards for street cleaning were appallingly low even in London, and the Stratford authorities may have chosen to make an example of a man somewhat more careless than the rest.

Tradition and Fact.

Perhaps the tradition that he was a butcher has operated unfavourably in certain ways in our conception of his endowments and dignity. On the other hand, we know by the town records that he served first as alderman, then as mayor or bailiff, and after that, as chief alderman of Stratford; also that he enjoyed for more than thirty years the distinction of being called " Mr." in the town records and elsewhere. He must have commanded the respect of his fellow townsmen for his judgment in matters of the law, even though they sometimes visited the law upon him. His appreciation of the drama is suggested by the fact that he was the first Stratford bailiff to give London players an official welcome to the town, and during his term of office, when the poet was only four years of age, two London companies of actors were entertained by the Stratford Corporation.

His financial condition was evidently subject to many fluctuations. His wife's property had given him a substantial beginning and by the time that his son William was about eleven years of age, he had acquired at least two houses in Stratford. At one time he is set down as having paid twelve pence, a very creditable sum, towards the salary of the parish beadle; but a little later his fortunes dropped so low that he could not pay the fourpence, due from him as alderman, for the poor, and, if tradition is to be trusted, he took William away from school to work towards the family support. During this middle period he was forced to mortgage one of the properties gained through his wife, and to surrender another, both much to his grief; and later records tell of how one of his creditors, who had obtained permission to levy on his goods, reported that he could find nothing on which a levy could be made. There must have been a return to his old prosperity after this, however; for, at his death in 1601, he left to the poet the two houses on Henley Street which he had long before owned, and there were other signs that his fortunes had mended.

Tradition.

There is a pleasant tradition,[1] that a certain still un-discovered Sir John Mennes who saw him once in his shop, called him "a merry-cheeked old man," and heard him say that "Will was a good honest fellow," though he himself "durst have crackt a jeast [jest] with him at any time." This, if Sir John and his statement could both be authenticated, would throw a genial light on a nature apt to be dismissed as contentious and irascible. Altogether, he must have been a man of intelligence, versatility, and breadth of view, and his somewhat paradoxical combination of qualities furnished his son with a more promising inheritance than the steady-going mediocrity of his fellow law-makers could have provided.

Evidence as to Shakespeare's Life.

Facts.

There are only four fully proved facts about Shake-

[1] Sir Sidney Lee in a later edition of his *Life of Shakespeare* argues seriously for the acceptance of the testimony involved and adds some details; although the claim must still rest upon evidence without right to be called documentary.

33. SHAKESPEARE'S BIRTHPLACE, IN 1807.

34. BIBLE OF SHAKESPEARE'S AND PARISH REGISTER.
With Page open at the Entry of Shakespeare's Birth.

speare, until he is thirty years old. These four are the register of his baptism, a record concerned with his

1564

35. FACSIMILE OF ENTRY OF SHAKESPEARE'S BIRTH IN THE PARISH REGISTER.

marriage, the register of the birth of his oldest daughter, and that of the twins, Hamnet and Judith. All the

36. THE HOUSE IN HENLEY STREET IN WHICH SHAKESPEARE WAS BORN.

rest that passes for biography during that period is unproved tradition or, at best, reasonable conjecture. A fair proportion of this remainder is, however, accepted by scholars as having some show of probability.

Shakespeare's baptism is entered on the register of the parish church of Stratford with the date of April 26, 1564, and it is inferred that he was born on April 22 or 23, allowing the usual interval between birth and baptism. This approximate dating is supported by the statement on his gravestone, that he was fifty-two years old when he died on April 23, 1616. It must be remembered, of course, that the difference between counting calendar time in those days and ours would throw the poet's birthday early in May of our calendar. Scholars have been content, as a rule, to leave the traditional April 23 as the popular one for celebrating Shakespeare's birthday; but at the time of a special Shakespeare pageant it might not be amiss to attempt a more accurate date.

Boyhood.

Conjecture.

There are, of course, various probabilities as to the life of any Stratford youth of Shakespeare's time. That he attended the Stratford grammar school between the years 1571 and 1577 seems natural enough, as that would cover the period between his eighth and his fourteenth year. If he did so, then Walter Roche was his schoolmaster and later on possibly Thomas Hunt. Educational treatises of the time suggest that he would have studied at the grammar school much Latin grammar and selections from many Latin au-

thors, among them Seneca, Terence, Cicero, etc. His
quotations in *Love's Labour's Lost* of certain Latin
phrases found in the Latin grammar used in the public

37.   THE GUILD OF THE HOLY CROSS, STRATFORD.

schools of that day seem to prove his acquaintance with
that book.   His easy playing upon French words in
one of the scenes of *Henry V* suggests a comfortable
knowledge of French, whether he gained it at school

38. ROOM IN WHICH SHAKESPEARE WAS BORN.

39. INNER ROOM IN SHAKESPEARE'S BIRTHPLACE.

or not; for although the sources of his play gave him the hint for such humour he heightens it with a dextrous hand.   He had Latin enough, too, for his practical needs, although Ben Jonson's curt comment that Shakespeare knew " small Latin and less Greek " is probably just by any exacting standards; indeed there is no real evidence that he knew Greek at all.   He was certainly conversant with popular Italian fiction later on, but he probably acquired all his knowledge of this by reading in London to meet the demands of his playwriting, and there is no proof that he had any close knowledge of the Italian language, as the Italian sources of his plays were available in translation.

Tradition.

Nothing attests his attendance at the Kenilworth festivities in honour of Elizabeth in 1575, although it seems likely enough that, if conditions were even half favourable to his going the short journey of fifteen miles, he would not lightly have missed the going, boy of eleven as he was.   Proof is lacking, too, for the tradition that his father took him, at thirteen, from school to help in his business as butcher.

Conjecture.

Critics tend now to the belief that his father was a greengrocer rather than a butcher and there is some possibility that he was a glover as well; but the stories gather about the butcher's calling.   We can only smile at the tale of how the prospective dramatist, when he killed a calf for his father's shop, would " doe it in a high style and make a speech "; or at that other, of the rival butcher's son, who " was held not at all inferior to him for a naturall wit, his acquaintance and coetanean [contemporary] but dyed young," thus discreetly waiving the burden of proof.

Marriage.
Facts.

For the year when Shakespeare was eighteen, 1582, there is a bond signed by two farmers of Shottery, a

40. ANNE HATHAWAY'S BIRTHPLACE.

neighbouring hamlet, relieving the Bishop of Worcester and his subordinates from all responsibility for

allowing unusual haste in the marriage of William
Shakespeare and Anne Hathaway. The bond shows
that Shakespeare was eight years younger than his
bride and suggests that although the marriage was being hastened by her friends, the parents of the groom
may have had no knowledge of its occurrence, their
names not appearing, as would be customary, with

41. KITCHEN IN SHAKESPEARE'S BIRTHPLACE.

the marriage of a minor. Six months later, in 1583,
the baptism of a daughter, Susannah, is entered upon
the register of the Stratford church; and two years
later, in 1585, that of the twins, Hamnet and Judith.
There were apparently no other children.

After the birth of the three children there is another
long gap in recorded facts. Tradition fills in the gap
with various stories explaining why he left Stratford,
how he was occupied on his first departure, and what

fortune befell him when he first went to London. All of this must, however, be considered unproved, whatever the probability.

Tradition.

The most widespread of all the current Warwickshire traditions of Shakespeare to-day is the one which connects his name with the Falcon Inn at the village of Bidford, about ten miles from Stratford. The story is given here as related by a Warwickshire workman familiar with Bidford and all the country around — this modern version seeming more interesting as showing the persistence of the tradition than any older one which is too new to be authentic. The tale runs that one Saturday night, before Shakespeare's first departure to London, he was returning from a drinking bout, and stopped at the Falcon Tavern at Bidford to sleep off his drunkenness and continue on his way home the next day. He gained permission from the host of the Falcon, " for a consideration," to pass the summer night under a crabtree in front of the inn; but his stupor was so heavy that he slept two nights instead of one, and when he awoke on Monday morning, he saw the people busy in the fields at the plough. When he called out to know why they were ploughing on Sunday, they told him what had happened. " Then they reckoned Shakespeare laughed to die," and not only that, but he improvised the well-known rhyme about the neighboring villages in which he had been at different times overcome:

> Piping Pebworth, dancing Marston,
> Haunted Hillboro, hungry Grafton,

Dodging Exhall, popish Wexford,
Beggarly Broom, and drunken Bidford.

It might be added that the narrator of this version
told it to illustrate Shakespeare's honesty, declaring
that, of his own accord, the poet paid the host of the
Falcon Inn more than he had promised, when he found
that he had slept two nights instead of one.

Leaving Stratford.
Tradition.

Over-frequent poaching in the deer park of Sir
Thomas Lucy is usually given as the cause for Shakespeare's leaving Stratford, as he apparently did about
1586; to this reason is often added the further one that
a loveless marriage to a woman too old to make him
happy doubled his motives for escape. The loveless
marriage has never been incontrovertibly proved, and
it is said in Stratford that the authorities are forbidding the repetition by the tourist guides of the story of
the deer stealing, because they do not accept it as
authentic. This in itself means much in a place where
so many traditions about Shakespeare are thoroughly
commercialised as facts. Another tradition was
passed on in 1693 by a Stratford parish clerk who was
born before Shakespeare's death. He reported that
the poet " fled from the town to escape a butcher to
whom he had been apprenticed "; but there is nothing
convincing to commend this tale, although the deer-
stealing story is not so easily dismissed.

The earliest account of the poaching comes from

42. STRATFORD-ON-AVON, AS IT IS TO-DAY.

43. FRANCIS BEAUMONT.   44. JOHN FLETCHER.

45. THE SHAKESPEARE JUBILEE CELEBRATION AT STRATFORD.

46. FULKE GREVILLE, LORD   47. NATHANIEL FIELD,
     BROOKE.   THE ACTOR.

a seventeenth-century vicar who declared that Shakespeare was given to stealing both rabbits and venison, especially from Sir Thomas Lucy; and that this knight, after having him often whipped for his misbehaviour, drove him away from his native town. A later writer adds that, after Sir Thomas Lucy's earlier punishments, which Shakespeare felt to be unjustly severe, he wrote a bitter ballad about the knight, and so brought upon himself fiercer penalties than ever, and took refuge from them in flight from Stratford. This second story seems important only as showing how tradition may grow. More serious critics have, however, found in the Justice Shallow of *King Henry IV*

48. SIR THOMAS
LUCY.

and of *The Merry Wives of Windsor* a satirical portrait of Sir Thomas Lucy, citing especially Shallow's treatment of poaching as a star chamber offence, and the apparent allusion to the Lucy coat-of-arms. On the other hand, it has been denied that Sir Thomas Lucy had anywhere in the vicinity of Stratford a deer-park in which Shakespeare could have committed his depredations, and shown that there was very little in common, even for purposes of caricature, between Sir Thomas Lucy, the sterling and honoured Puritan knight and magistrate, and the pretentious and emptyheaded country justice presented in Shallow. It is argued from this that no audience could have grasped the resemblance, even if Shakespeare himself had intended to suggest it; and that he would never have outraged fairness and public estimates in such a misrepresentation of a noble man. Neither side is entirely convincing. It is conceivable that if Shakespeare was forced to leave Stratford on account of punishments which he felt to be unjust, he might have chosen to put into a play a thrust or two at the causer of this injustice, whether he expected the thrust to be fully understood by his audience or not; he might even have enjoyed a certain amount of irrelevance in the character chosen to express his resentment against the Warwickshire magistrate. On the other hand, the deer-stealing episode is entirely unsupported by actual proofs and especially on this account, is too picturesque to be convincing.

Arrival in London.

Tradition.

Conjecture tends to place Shakespeare's arrival in London between the years 1586 and 1588. There is a tradition that he did not go directly to the metropolis, but " was for a time a schoolmaster in the country "; and another that once arrived in London, he drifted quickly towards the public theatres. The claim that he was a schoolmaster is entirely unsupported, but the other tradition is very generally acknowledged as probable, being encouraged both by known facts of Shakespeare's life and by the persistent testimony of a suc-

cession of writers, who vary in their versions, but keep
to the same general claim.   The earliest declared that
he was " received into the playhouse as a servitor and
by this means had an opportunity to be what he afterwards proved."   A second tells us that he began by
holding horses outside the theatre for those who had
come on horseback to the performance; another that
he served first as call-boy and so gained his impetus
towards acting and dramatic composition.

The possibility that he began by holding horses outside the theatre is made plausible by several facts.   The
only two public theatres existing in London on his arrival, if he reached there in 1586, were situated outside the city limits at a distance which made riding
there the custom of people of means.   Also both playhouses, the Theatre and the Curtain, were under the
management of James Burbage, who was the owner of
a livery.   Also it would have been natural enough for
him to use one business to help the other, and in doing
this, to find it convenient to employ various youths as
assistants for holding the horses around the theatre.
It is known, too, that in 1587 three London companies
of actors visited Stratford, and, as has been more than
once suggested, some word of anxiety from his father
or some interested friend at home may have influenced
one or more of the actors towards giving the Stratford
youth a start in a great city.   The tradition of Shakespeare's early contact with these London theatres is supported by his later identification with other theatres

under the same management, that of the Burbage family.[2]   It is highly natural of course, that, failing any definite knowledge of Shakespeare's early doings in London, imaginative biographers should have surmised his beginning in surroundings where he is discovered a few years later in such successful and varied activity.   This possibility must not, however, be confused with proof, and Dr. Johnson's story that Shakespeare's success in the business of holding horses led to the organisation of a group of horseboys as " Shakespeare's boys " can only be dismissed with amusement.

Conjecture.

For the year 1592 there are two published allusions thought by most critics to refer to Shakespeare.   One occurs in *Greene's Groats worth of Witte bought with a Million of Repentance* which was written by Robert Greene the dramatist and published soon after his death.   In it he attacks very savagely some actor-playwright whom he accuses of succeeding by stealing from others' plays; and his attack seems to involve a pun on Shakespeare's name, and a parody on a line found both in *3 Henry VI* and in an older play on which it is based.   If the allusion by Greene was to Shakespeare it shows that within approximately seven years after he was last heard of in Stratford, the latter

[2] It is known that by 1596, probably by 1593 or 1594, he was living in Bishopsgate near Shoreditch, the site of the Burbage theatres and that by 1598 he had moved across the river to the Bankside, obviously in order to be within the more recent theatrical centre.

had become successful both as a playwright and as an actor. That same year, after Greene's pamphlet had given offence to the one chiefly attacked, its editor,

49. ROBERT GREENE IN HIS SHROUD.
(From Dickenson's "Greene in Conceipt,"
1598.)

Henry Chettle, apologised in print for having published the attack upon one so little deserving it, and declared:

"I am as sorry as if the originall fault had beene my fault, because myselfe have seene his demeanour no less civill than he excelent in the qualitie [i.e. the calling of an actor] he professes."

Chettle testified, too, to the playwright's good name for fair dealing and to the admiration which his writing has aroused. All that he implied seems borne out by later testimonies of contemporaries as to Shakespeare's personality and there is no other actor-playwright of the time to whom the two allusions might, in general, so fitly apply. There is therefore a very reasonable probability that they were meant to refer to Shakespeare. If they were, Shakespeare must have been busy both as an actor and as a playwright by 1592.

First Authentic Emergence in London.

In 1593 Shakespeare's first non-dramatic poem, *Venus and Adonis,* was published under his own name by the same Richard Field who had preceded him to London and risen high in his calling as printer. The poem became popular at once, and added one more phase to Shakespeare's artistic activity. In the following year he published his *Lucrece* and took his place as one of the most acceptable writers of the love poetry of the day. That he felt a special pride in the achievement of these poems is suggested by the care with which he guided them through the press, although he had apparently no interest in the correct editing of his plays.

Relation to the Earl of Southampton.

Both poems were dedicated to the Earl of Southampton, one of the most courted of all the younger nobility. Whether the first dedication was a pure venture on Shakespeare's part is uncertain; although

50.   SIR WALTER RALEIGH AND HIS ELDEST SON.

51. HENRY WRIOTHESLEY, THIRD EARL OF SOUTHAMPTON.
From the original picture at Welbeck Abbey.

we know from Spenser's mention of a certain unau-
thorised dedication to Sir Philip Sidney that such
public suing to people of power was not to be under-
taken rashly. In any case the tone of modest hope-
fulness which marks the first dedication does credit
to Shakespeare's self-respect:

" Right Honourable:

"I know not how I shall offend in dedicating my un-
polished lines to your lordship, nor how the world will
censure me for choosing so strong a prop to support so
weak a burden; only if your honour seem but pleased, I
account myself highly praised, and vow to take advantage
of all idle hours till I have honoured you with some graver
favour. . . .

                    "Your honour's in all duty,
                        "WILLIAM SHAKESPEARE."

The young earl must have received Shakespeare's
offering with very friendly cordiality, whether he had
encouraged its bestowal or not; for the second dedication shows a firmer confidence and even a tone of
affection.

" The love I dedicate to your lordship is without end;
where-of this pamphlet without beginning is but a superfluous moiety. The warrant I have of your honourable disposition, not the worth of my untutored lines, makes it assured of acceptance."

Southampton is the only patron with whose name
Shakespeare's has ever been associated by any agreement of scholars and if, as some conjecture, he was the
young nobleman celebrated in the sonnets, he becomes

the patron of all Shakespeare's non-dramatic poetry.
It would be worth much to know just how significant
and personal the relation between the two men was;
and one can well believe that, however limited the
contact, the good will and encouragement of a man so
far above him in the eyes of the world must have meant
much to Shakespeare in the years when he was beginning to be known.

Tradition.

There is a pleasant story of how Southampton
proved his friendship for Shakespeare in a practical
way, and although no evidence of its truth has been
discovered, it shows at least how the friendly attitude
of Southampton became the basis for anecdote and
illustration.

"There is one instance so singular in the magnificence of
this patron of Shakespeare's that if I had not been assured
that the story was handed down by Sir William D'Avenant
[who lived in Shakespeare's lifetime and is said to have
claimed to be his natural son] who was probably very well
acquainted with his affairs, I should not venture to have
inserted, that my Lord Southampton at one time gave him a
thousand pounds to enable him to go through with a pur-
chase which he heard he had a mind to: a bounty very great
and very rare at any time."

Financial Successes.

It is a striking fact that although Shakespeare's
native endowment and success were probably much
more in the direction of playwriting than of acting, his

income came chiefly from his calling as an actor. Sir
Sidney Lee, one of his more recent biographers, estimates that even before 1599 Shakespeare was receiving a yearly income of about £150, or £1040 in terms of
to-day. Of this amount only about one-eighth would
have come from his plays, and all the rest from his

52. THE FALCON TAVERN, BANKSIDE.
The Resort of Shakespeare and His Brother Poets

connection with the theatre as actor, except some possible returns from the non-dramatic poems. From
1599 on, his income was much larger because of his
proprietary share in the Globe theatre. The Globe
is said to have been capable of accommodating about
2000 spectators and its annual profits in Shakespeare's

time are estimated to have been about £8000, by
modern count about £64,000. The profits of the Globe
were divided among sixteen shareholders, of whom
Shakespeare was one of the larger. Later on he was
a sharer, too, in the profits of the Blackfriars theatre, and may have received as much as £100 annually

from that. His plays were delivered directly to his company to be
acted, and the money he received
for them was from their use in
this way, not from their publication.

There is good reason to believe
that while Shakespeare was making his fame and fortune in London he was keeping in close touch
with Stratford. The death of his
only son, Hamnet, in 1596, must
have struck a pitiless blow at some
of his hopes, for everything points
to his ambition to build up a
strong position for his family in
Stratford; but in that very year

**53. SHAKESPEARE'S
CREST AND COAT-
OF-ARMS.**

John Shakespeare, his father, applied for a coat-
of-arms,[3] probably at the poet's instigation and expense; and the Stratford records show a steady ac-

---

[3] The coat-of-arms is described as "Gold, on a bend sable, a
spear of the first, and for his crest or cognisance a falcon, his
wings displayed argent, standing on a wreath of his colours, supporting a spear gold steeled as aforesaid. Motto—*Non sans
Droit.*"

quisition of property there by the poet himself.   The
coat-of-arms was granted after a delay which has recently been found connected with interesting complaints over the social ambi-
tions of actors.[4]   In 1597
Shakespeare purchased New
Place, the largest private
dwelling in Stratford.   Four
years later he inherited from
his father the two houses on
Henley Street,[5] and   still
later he acquired another residence and a tract of land,
and bought up the right to
collect certain taxes known
as tithes.   He may have developed also, either then or
earlier, important business
interests connected with the
sale of malt, although the
fact that there were several
William   Shakespeares   in
Stratford during his ma-
turer years makes certain

54.   HOUSE IN HIGH STREET,
STRATFORD.
Erected 1596

phases of this question difficult to decide.   He had
property, too, in London, and was clearly interested in

[4] Sir Sidney Lee in the latest edition of his *Life of William
Shakespeare* discusses this in very interesting detail.

[5] One of these is known to-day as the birthplace and the other
as his father's shop; but very little of the original material of
the houses may be considered to be still in existence.

business as such, besides desiring the advantages which financial success would bring. It seems easy to detect a great personal ambition to go back to Stratford as a gentleman of substance and influence; for he steadily

55. STRATFORD COLLEGE, PROPERTY OF JOHN COMBE.

followed the course which would bring this about, living with amazing thrift and modesty in London while he piled up at home the marks of his prosperity.

Human Relationships.

Records have recently been found of a law suit which gives us our best light upon Shakespeare in the natural social relationships of life. They show that about 1598 he was living in London in the home of a French Huguenot wig-maker, Christopher Mountjoy. Mountjoy had also taken into his household a youth, Stephen Bellott, who, after a year, was bound over to him as apprentice in wig-making for a term of five years; and the term was worked out with great satisfaction on both sides. At the end of that time Bellott, through the master's kindness, went to travel in

56. RICHARD BURBAGE.

Shakespeare's Friend
and Fellow Actor.

57. EDWARD ALLEYN,

Actor and Founder of
Dulwich College.

58. QUEEN ELIZABETH, 1558–1603.
From a painting belonging to the University of
Cambridge.

59. EDMUND SPENSER.

60. THE EARL OF LEICESTER

61. QUEEN ELIZABETH.

From the King of England's collection in St. James' Palace.

Spain, and when he returned, received, through Shake-speare, Mountjoy's offer of the hand of his only daugh-ter, Mary — a generous dowry being promised if the marriage came about. There had already been much "shewe of good will" between Mary and Stephen; so the marriage was accomplished and, as far as the young people themselves were concerned, seems to have been happy enough. The father of Mary, how-ever, Christopher Mountjoy, apparently repented his promises in regard to the dowry, and at the end of six years Stephen brought suit against him for failure to fulfil them, claiming that the contract had been for £50 in money and various movable prop-erties. The case seems not to have been tried openly in the courts, but questions were sent to various wit-nesses and written testimonies required in reply. Among these witnesses was Shakespeare, named in the documents as "William Shakespeare of Strat-ford-upon-Avon in the county of Warwick, gentleman, of the age of 46 or thereabout." Out of his testi-mony and that of the others comes a picture of his genial, helpful attitude towards a family of humble sort, with whom accident may have thrown him as a lodger. His friendly interest in the love affairs of Stephen and Mary while the marriage is being ar-ranged, his guarded references to all in his testimony, and the kindness with which he avoids offending either father-in-law or son-in-law, so angrily pitted against each other then, suggest the social qualities in him which would make friendships easy. There are evidences of his befriending Stratford people, too, either in London or at home.

Tradition.

One story of his kindly attitude towards those needing help is involved in the tradition of his aid to a fellow dramatist who was not yet underway. As it stands, it may certainly not be accepted for fact, but it is one of several traditions which show the general belief in Shakespeare's kindness of heart and, even as pure tradition, it helps to explain the warmth of feeling which Chettle had shown in 1592 in speaking of Shakespeare's good qualities as a man. The story runs as follows:

"His [i.e. Shakespeare's] acquaintance with Ben Jonson began with a remarkable piece of humanity and good nature. Mr. Jonson, who was at that time altogether unknown to the world, had offered one of his plays to the players in order to have it acted, and the persons into whose hands it was put, after having turned it carelessly and superciliously over, were just returning it to him with an ill-natured answer that it would be of no service to their company, when Shakespeare luckily cast his eye upon it, and found something so well in it as to engage him first to read it through, and afterwards to recommend Mr. Jonson and his writing to the public."

It is interesting to combine with this unauthenticated story the testimony of Jonson himself to Shakespeare's natural kindness and to his own affection for him:

" I loved the man and do honour to his memory on this side idolatry as much as any. He was indeed honest, and of an open and free nature," etc.

Retirement to Stratford.

Conjecture.

It is not certain when Shakespeare began in Stratford his life of the gentleman of means and of leisure. The year 1611 is apt to be given as the date, but he may have been collaborating with Fletcher in London after this time, and we hear of his activities there in connection with city property which he owned. Indeed it was in 1613 that he acquired a property in the Blackfriars district. This makes it seem probable that he withdrew by degrees from the contact and interests which had bound him to London. He was well equipped to live the Stratford life which he coveted; for his wealth, reputation, and coat-of-arms must all have combined to make him an imposing figure in the quiet town and he evidently accepted his full responsibility to prove himself a public-spirited citizen there. He had apparently retired from active service on the stage several years before his return to Stratford, and if he still worked upon dramatic composition after his return, it was apparently only to the extent of writing parts of *Henry VIII,* and of *The Two Noble Kinsmen;* all the other plays associated with his name being assigned by critics to an earlier date. That a man of Shakespeare's vigour of mind and power of creative imagination should thus have laid down his work be-

fore he was fifty years old is a surprising fact, and one
not to be explained by our present knowledge; although
it is easy to believe that Stratford offered him many al-
lurements after all his years of striving and success
in London; and there are many evidences that the
management of so many properties as he owned might
have constituted an occupation in itself. One of the
diversions of these more quiet years in Stratford has
come to light in the *Household Book of Belvoir Castle,*
where his name appears for the year 1613, in connection with that of his fellow actor, Burbage, in the
record of payment for the making of a heraldic device.
The device was worn by the Earl of Rutland in a
tournament at court, and it appears that Shakespeare's
part was the working out of the emblem; Burbage's,
that of painting and gilding the device. For their
work they received jointly £4 8s, of which 14s fell to
the poet's share. The incident throws a pleasant
light on the great actor and the great dramatist divert-
ing themselves together with an artistic venture apart
from their callings, and turning an honest penny by
it as well. It is worth noting, too, that Southampton,
whose relations with Shakespeare have already been
discussed and the Earl of Rutland were close friends
and are both reputed to have been great lovers of the
theatre. Records, very recently brought to light, show
that later on Burbage, at least, was employed again
by Rutland for a similar service. In the record of the
first transaction the title *Mr.* is prefixed to Shakespeare's name, but not to that of Burbage.

Family Ties.
Facts.

Shakespeare's father had died, as already said, in 1601, and his mother's burial is recorded as occurring on September 9, 1608. His daughter, Susannah, had in 1607 married Dr. John Hall, a Stratford physician who became much renowned for his professional skill. He waited upon the neighbouring nobility, as well as upon humbler people, and his epitaph declares him "worthy by his deserts to surpass Nestor in years" and "most famed in medical art." That the epitaph did not exceed even the large privileges which epitaphs justly enjoy is shown by the fact that an account of various cures by him was published nearly twenty-five years after his death. He must have been a very satisfactory son-in-law to Shakespeare, both for his prestige as a physician and for his personal qualities, since it was to Hall and his wife that Shakespeare left with much confidence the right to administer his estate.

His second son-in-law, Thomas Quiney, married to Judith in the year of Shakespeare's death, was less distinguished and apparently less favoured by the poet. Some degree of culture in Quiney is suggested by his having been master of the Stratford grammar school for a time, possibly also by his having held the position of parish clerk. At the time of his marriage he seems to have been a vintner and wine merchant, and the parish register shows that he was four years younger than his bride, he being twenty-seven and Judith thirty-one.

Death.

Shakespeare made his will early in 1516, the year of his death; but whether he was apprehensive of the end or not, the will declared that he was in perfect health.   He revised it in some of its details and signed

1616

Aprill

25 | with Shakspeare gent X

62.   FACSIMILE OF ENTRY OF SHAKESPEARE'S BURIAL IN THE PARISH REGISTER.

it in March.   He died the next month at the very early age of fifty-two, and the parish register records his burial on April 25.

Tradition.

There is no authentic clue to the illness which carried him off, although a later Stratford parson recorded the town report that he died of a fever caused by " a merry meeting " with Ben Jonson and Michael Drayton, who had presumably come to visit him in Stratford.

Fact.

The exact date of Shakespeare's death is indicated on the tombstone as April 23, by the old style of dating, but like that of his birthday would fall early in May if set by our modern calendar. He was honoured with a burial place in the chancel of the church and

GOOD FREND FOR IESVS SAKE FORBEARE,
TO DIGG THE DVST ENCLOASED HEARE:
BLESTE BE Y MAN Y SPARES TIES STONES,
AND CVRST BE HEY MOVES MY BONES.

63.   INSCRIPTION ON SHAKESPEARE'S TOMB.

the well-known forbidding lines were set over his tomb.

Tradition.

The authorship of the lines is unknown, but their sentiment seems to have been accepted about Stratford as Shakespeare's own.   There is a tradition, easy to believe, that although his wife and daughters " did earnestly desire to be leyd in the same grave with him," they dared not gratify their desire.

The Will.

The will contains many items of human interest. The " second-best bed with the furniture " [6] is the only bequest named for his wife and includes his only mention of her.   This has provided scholars with gloomy

[6] The word furniture apparently denotes the belongings of the bed.

confirmations of the accepted view that Shakespeare's
marriage was an unhappy one. To Judith he be-
queathed money in somewhat moderate proportions,
but to Susannah and Dr. Hall, her husband, lands,
houses in Stratford and beyond, and most of his
" goodes, chattels, leases, jewels, household stuffe,"
etc. The will is full of business energy and clear-cut
discriminations, and provides abundant testimony both
to Shakespeare's wealth and to his social relationships.
One of his bequests to Susannah, as executor, names
" all my barnes, stables, orchards, gardens, landes, tene-
mentes, and hereditaments [inherited property] what-
soever scituat, lyeing and being, or to be had, receyved,
perceyved, or taken, within the townes, hamletes, villages, fieldes and groundes, of Stratford upon Avon,
Oldstratford, Bushopton and Welcombe, or in anie of
them in the saied countie of Warr " [Warwickshire],
etc.

There are generous remembrances for a sister and
her children, legacies for buying rings for neighbourhood friends and fellow actors — among the latter,
Burbage and the later publishers of the First Folio,
Heminge and Condell.

The careful instructions as to the disposition of his
landed possessions, and the concentration of them upon
the oldest daughter and upon her children, suggests
the desire to hold his estate together as long as possible, even though no son was left to carry on the
name.

Dramatic Composition.

Definite proof of Shakespeare's writing of plays does not appear until 1598 when Francis Meres, who may perhaps be described as a literary critic, mentions a critical work not only Shakespeare's *Sonnets* as being known among his private friends, but his success in tragedy and comedy. He names six of Shakespeare's plays of each type, as already known to the stage: "*Two Gentlemen of Verona,* his *Errors,* his *Love Labours Lost,* his *Love Labours Wonne,* his *Midsummers Night Dream,* and his *Merchant of Venice*" for comedy; and, "for tragedy his *Richard the 2, Richard the 8, Henry the 4, King John, Titus Andronicus* and his *Romeo and Juliet.*" After 1599, allusions to the plays multiply rapidly, and there are various indications that Shakespeare was high in reputation as a dramatist within ten or twelve years after leaving Stratford; also that until 1611 he showed a fair regularity in producing two plays a year.

As Actor.

As an actor he is known to have taken part in two comedies given before Queen Elizabeth in 1594 at the Christmas season and in 1596 his name appears along with those of others of his company in a petition to be allowed to improve the Blackfriars playhouse. He is named second among the members of his company when James I makes it "The King's company" in 1603, and is mentioned as one of the nine members of the company to whom the scarlet livery was given for their appearance as the King's servants on the occasion of the royal entry into London in the following year. He is known to have had part in Jonson's *Everyman in his Humour* at times between 1598 and 1603, and to have played in *Sejanus* in 1603. There is no proof of his having acted after this.

Tradition.

There is a tradition of his having played the part of Adam in *As You Like It,* and, in general, the parts of old men. There is little or no evidence, however, in support of this tradition.

Spelling of the Name.

Stratford records of Shakespeare's time show the poet's family name spelled in sixteen different ways: Shakespeare himself seems to have used three different spellings, possibly a fourth as well. Modern scholarship favours the longest form of the name because Shakespeare used it in his signature to the dedicatory letters to *Venus and Adonis,* and in that to *Lucrece* — poems which he evidently put carefully through the press himself; also it appears in the First Folio edition of his works, on the title pages of most of the plays printed separately in his lifetime, and in most of the legal documents in which the name appears. It would therefore seem that this was the more formal and exact spelling and that the shorter renderings were the result of carelessness or haste.

Portraits.

The Stratford Bust.

Shakespeare's personal appearance is still the ground of much debate. Several portraits with some claim to authenticity are in existence, but none of them is known to have been done in Shakespeare's lifetime. The bust on the monument in the Stratford church where Shakespeare is buried is thought by many to have been made from a death mask, because of a certain rigidity of expression.[7] The crude workmanship may be partly to blame for this, however, as it was made by a stone cutter, not by a skilled artist. It was coloured at first; then, later on, imperfectly white-washed, and later still restored, as far as possible, to its original colouring, of which some marks remained. It is dignified and thoughtful but unsatisfying. So far as is known it is the oldest existing likeness.

The Droeshout Engraving.

Next to it in importance is the engraving used as a frontispiece in the First Folio edition of Shakespeare's works in 1623. This could not have been made in Shakespeare's lifetime because the engraver, Martin Droeshout, was only seven years old when Shakespeare died. It, too, seems inadequate and uninteresting in

[7] It is to be remembered that this book goes to press before recent discoveries which have been announced by Sir Sidney Lee as bearing on the history of the Stratford monument have been made available.

spite of Jonson's lines testifying to its faithfulness as a likeness.

The Flower Portrait.

Another portrait,[8] discovered recently by a Stratford citizen, Mr. Charles Flower, has been called by some the model for the First Folio engraving. It hangs in the Shakespeare Memorial Picture Gallery in Stratford and is painted on a plank panel, being inscribed with the date 1609. This, if authentic, would make its workmanship date from seven years before Shakespeare's death, but there is no general acceptance either of this date for it, or of the claim that it served as a model for the Droeshout [8] engraving. It has, however, a striking similarity to the latter.

Tradition.

Other well-known portraits are the Ely portrait,[9] once owned by the Bishop of Ely and, on the whole, the most gratifying in its suggestions; the Chandos,[10] somewhat objectionable, especially because of the earrings, but said by tradition to have been painted by Shakespeare's fellow actor, Joseph Taylor. Whether this is true or not — and the claim seems very improbable — the picture was owned first by Davenant, then by Betterton, the great Shakespearean actor, and later by Mrs. Barry. Other famous likenesses, either actual or alleged, are the Garrick Club bust, the death mask, the Clarendon portrait, etc.

[8] Opposite.   [9] Facing p. 68.   [10] Facing p. 69.

PORTRAITS OF SHAKESPEARE.
64. The Droeshout Engraving (above) and (65.) the so-called
Flower Portrait (below).

Gerard Honthorst.

66. BEN JONSON.

67. MICHAEL DRAYTON.

Out of all this collection of portraits, busts, etc., with their confusing differences, emerge a few harmonious impressions as to Shakespeare's personal appearance. They visualise him for us in a general way as having a head of ample proportions, hair full about the ears but scanty at the top, thoughtful eyes, and a dignity of bearing which would bring respect. None of them suggests the conviviality or gayer sense of companionship accredited to him by tradition, although one can discover in all the portraits justice and kindness in human relationships. The suggestion is of the judicial temperament, too, rather than of the imaginative: altogether one must conclude that either Shakespeare was a bad subject for portrait makers, or that none of the likenesses which survive is based closely on his actual appearance.

If we try to summarise our assets for acquaintance with the life of Shakespeare it becomes clear that a large mass of the material usually accepted as biography must be treated only as tradition, much of it as tradition of an improbable sort. On the other hand, records from the court, legal documents of many kinds, reference by contemporary writers, information available from the publication of his own poems or plays, parish records, and many other aids, furnish a surprising amount of reliable testimony as to his life and human relationships — an amount which probably bulks as large as that which remains to us about any other Elizabethan dramatist.

V

SHAKESPEARE'S PLAYS

Shakespeare's Dramatic Inheritance.

THE religious plays, the chief heritage of Elizabethan drama, left a strong impression upon the mind
of Shakespeare. They touched both his imagination
and his sense of humour, as is shown by his repeated
allusions to them; also, many of his minor characters
bear the strong impress of the morality figures. From
the secular dramatists who were writing when he began his work, he learned far more. In a very definite
sense he went to school to them all — especially to
Marlowe, Lyly, and Kyd; and it is easy to see that he
is often following one or more of them closely in
dramatic method as well as in the details of literary
style — Lyly, especially in *Love's Labour's Lost* and
other light comedies; Kyd, in his work upon *Titus
Andronicus;* Marlowe, in *Richard II,* etc. He had a
real inheritance, too, from the court entertainments
which preceded his dramatic activity — those which
the court devised for itself in the way of pageants,
triumphs, etc., as well as the many kinds provided
from the outside. These were often childlike in conception and lacking in dramatic organisation, but they

68. THE BUST IN PROFILE.

69. BRINGING IN THE DEER.

This picture, one of the twelve painted in the Memorial Theatre at Stratford-on-Avon, though modern, is a very accurate representation of Hunting Costumes of the Elizabethan Period.

70. SHOREDITCH CHURCH.

71. THE LESS FORMAL DANCING ABOUT THE MAY POLE.

quickened the popular taste and imagination for all forms of spectacular entertainment, and gave many suggestions as to stage values. Help was, of course, passed on to him, too, from the classical drama, both in tragedy and in comedy. One of his very early plays was derived closely from Plautus's comedy *Menæchmi;* but in tragedy he seems to have taken the Senecan influence more from Kyd's interpretation of it than from the classical drama itself.

His Dramatic Contemporaries.

Shakespeare came upon a new wave of dramatic impulse in the development of the Elizabethan drama. Useful as they were to him, Marlowe, Peele, Kyd, and Lyly had all probably ceased to write when he began to be known; and he belonged to a middle brotherhood which included Dekker, Heywood, Chapman, Ben Jonson, Beaumont and Fletcher, Webster, etc. There is nothing to indicate that he ever showed or felt his great superiority to other dramatists of his time; on the contrary, all traditions and facts suggest that his relations with them were those of cordial equality; that he was ready to acknowledge the best in others, and modest enough to be receptive to ideas from many who were his inferiors.

His Dramatic Art.

His development as a dramatic artist came in large measure from his realisation that the drama is primarily the art of the theatre, not of the closet. It

came too, in part, from his utilising freely all existing material — whether old plays, novels, history, or
other aids — and devoting his efforts to presenting
that material in the most effective dramatic form.   It
sharpened his wits in his days of apprenticeship for
him to have to improve upon the dialogue and situations in the plays which he revised, and it helped to
prepare him for more original work.   He began, too,
in his first original work, with plays which put slight
strain upon him for subtle characterisation or situation, and worked his way along gradually in his mastery of technique.

Besides all this, however, one of the important elements of his success was his consciousness of the
limitations of his stage and of his audience; and his
further consciousness of the exact powers of the actors
for whom he was writing.   That he kept the meagre
facilities of the stage in mind is shown in countless
ways.   A careful study, recently made, of each scene
of the play [1] shows that there is hardly one which
is not set either by direct statement or by description
within the dialogue.[2]   The same is true in regard to
the passage of time.

Chronology.

Two kinds of evidence have been used in the effort to discover the dates of composition of Shakespeare's plays, many of which are still uncertain.   The

[1] By Jean Fraser in 1913.   The study is still unpublished.
[2] Occasionally this is accomplished by a prologue or a choruses,
as in *Henry V.*

first kind is based on information or suggestion found outside the plays — as any allusion in contemporary writings of which the date is known, to one of the plays, whether the allusion is by direct mention, by quotation, by imitation, or by any of many other possible means. Such evidence is often only partially conclusive, because incomplete. Thus Francis Meres's mention in 1598, in his *Palladis Tamia,* of twelve of Shakespeare's plays shows that this number had already been written by that year, but furnishes nothing more exact as to date. The entry of one of the plays at a certain date in the Stationers' Register — an act giving it licence to be printed — is somewhat more useful in suggesting the date of actual composition; but this, too, is uncertain, because a play, unless pirated, was not usually printed as long as it was holding the stage successfully. Some plays are recorded as having been performed at court on a certain date and so the time is limited on one side. In some instances there are extant editions of the separate plays, with the dates of their publication on the title page, but again this does not prove with close accuracy the date of composition. So, with many other kinds of external evidence.

The internal evidence is of course gathered from the plays themselves. In some of them there are allusions to events, or to writings — by Shakespeare or others — of which the date is known. In the plays as a group there are indications as to Shakespeare's gradual changes in dramatic method, metrical character-

istics, literary qualities, etc.   These concern especially
his tendencies as to plot-making and characterisation
at different periods of his career — the changing proportions of rhyme, prose, blank verse, run-on and
end-stopped lines, of Alexandrines, short lines, ten-
syllabled lines, etc.   The general conclusions in regard
to them are that Shakespeare began with a fondness
to rhyme, prose, and end-stopped lines, but tended
towards a varied blank verse with run-on lines, also to
pauses within the lines, and a considerable proportion
of feminine endings, or unaccented, extra-final syllables.
There is, also, a marked development in his skill
in plotting and in the grasp and seriousness shown in
characterisation.   It would be misleading, however,
to conclude that his practice tended steadily in these
directions.   Some of the plays of his middle years of
composition involved comedy situations or others, in
which prose or rhyme were the most suitable form for
the dialogue.   Both in these years and later he had his
lapses, and his latest plays are almost universally con-
ceded to have been far below many earlier ones in all
the greater dramatic values.

The table of dates formulated by the editors of the
Tudor edition of Shakespeare is given here as one of
the safest and most recent guides in chronology.   It
summarises the results of all existing testimony as to
actual or approximate dates for the various plays and
classifies them as comedies, histories, and tragedies,
within four chronological periods into which it is
convenient to divide Shakespeare's work.

Periods	Comedies		Histories		Tragedies	
I	L. L. L.	1591	1 Hy. VI	1590–2		
	C. of E.	1591	2 Hy. VI	1590–2		
	T. G. of V.	1591–2	3 Hy. VI	1590–2		
			R. III	1593		
			K. J.	1593		
					T. And.	1593–4
II	M. N. D.	1594–5	R. II	1595	R. and J.	1594–5
	M. of V.	1595–6	1 Hy. IV	1597		
	T. of S.	1596–7	2 Hy. IV	1598		
	M. W. of W.	1598	Hy. V	1599	J. Cæs	1599
	M. Ado	1599				
	A. Y. L. I.	1599–1600				
	TW. N.	1601				
III	T. & C.	1601–2			Ham.	1602–3
	A. Well	1602			Oth.	1604
	Meas.	1603			Lear	1605–6
					Macb	1606
					T.of Ath.	1607
	Per.	1607–8			A. & C.	1607–8
					Cor.	1609
IV	Cymb.	1610				
	W. Tale	1611				
	Temp.	1611	Hy. VIII	1612		
	T. N. K.	1612–13				

Plays of which Shakespeare Was Only Partly the Author.

To most readers of the plays printed under Shakespeare's name the problems of authorship connected with them are unknown; but these problems are important and, for more than one reason, intricate.

A surprising proportion of the plays are Shakespeare's revisions of work by other dramatists. This is true of practically all the historical plays — the

Henry VI plays, *Richard III, Richard II, King John,
1 and 2, Henry IV*, even of *King Lear;* [3] also of *The
Taming of the Shrew*, probably of *Hamlet*, and of
others of the non-historical sort. In both types of
plays he draws upon his originals with a freedom that is
at times almost startling, if we forget that they were
in his own eyes revisions, and that he was a practical
playwright, working to furnish his theatres and company with plays which the public would approve. We
must remember, too, that it was the fashion of the
time — as it still is to a larger degree than is realised
by the uninitiated — for a dramatist to take his material wherever he could find it, and to draw upon his
contemporaries as well as upon his predecessors in the
drama, for what he could adapt and revise. To-day
the original author's right is protected by copyright,
but innumerable foreign dramatists allow their plays
to be re-written or adapted for audiences different in
nationality from those for whom the plays were first
written. Shakespeare apparently brought trouble
upon himself once — if we may accept Greene's violent
allusion as being to him — when he availed himself of
the originals of the *Henry VI* plays; but, as has already been shown, even Greene's editor and friend,
Henry Chettle, vindicated the one attacked and declared that no aspersion could rest on his fair dealing
with others. On the whole, too, as one compares

[3] It has been conjectured by some that he may have had some
part in the originals of the *Henry VI* plays, but this idea finds
little acceptance among scholars.

closely the original of such a play and Shakespeare's re-writing of it, allowing fully for his following the original at times to his own disadvantage the conviction grows that all of these plays have strong right to be known as Shakespeare's, because he has put his stamp upon each as a whole.

Another group in which critics give him only a part are those which he probably helped to complete or re-furbish, but which lack, to any degree, the stamp of his unifying authorship. *Titus Andronicus, Timon of Athens, Pericles,* and possibly *Troilus and Cressida* belong to this group — at least two authors being plainly discernible in all but the last, even though the parts of each in a given scene cannot always be clearly discriminated.

A third class of those probably only in part Shakespeare's includes *Henry VIII* and *The Two Noble Kinsmen.* Whether Shakespeare left them unfinished when he retired to Stratford, agreeing to have Fletcher complete them; whether he and Fletcher worked in collaboration upon one or both; or, finally, whether they were altered by Fletcher after Shakespeare had completed them — are all conjectures which have been entertained. The second seems the most probable.

It is not likely that we shall ever know to a certainty every line which Shakespeare contributed in all the revised, doubtful, or collaborated plays. No phase of Shakespearean study is more illuminating than a close comparison of one of his plays with the source play on which it is founded, and the Bankside edition of Shakespeare's plays has made such a comparison comfortably possible by printing many of Shakespeare's plays with the originals in parallel columns. Corresponding parts are placed opposite each other, in spite of long vacant spaces at times in one or the other column. This makes it possible to see as the reading progresses the points at which Shakespeare has omitted his original; and others, at which he has supplemented it; as well as the slighter alterations in phrase, metrical form, etc. Not all the problems of authorship can be submitted to tests like these, however. In some instances, as with *Hamlet,* the source play is not in existence; and there are other difficulties as well.

Stages in Shakespeare's Dramatic Work.

Edward Dowden, a modern Shakespearean scholar, is chiefly responsible for the most popular divisions of Shakespeare's dramatic work into four periods, each with a dominant impulse behind it. The fact that he described each by a striking title has probably had much to do with the popularity of his divisions, which may be appropriate in the main, but seem too sweeping and emphatic in their generalisations. More recently, scholars have been tending to shake themselves free from them. Professor Dowden names the four periods: "In the Workshop," "In the World," "In the Depths," and "On the Heights"; and seeks to bind Shakespeare's plays up very closely in their tone with certain events in his life. Facts in his biography do not bear out the claim.

A more recent writer than Professor Dowden, Mr. E. H. C. Oliphant, names these four stages in Shakespeare's work:

(1) One in which he assisted some dramatist and, under his instruction, may have revised old plays of established reputation, and ventured some original efforts as well.

(2) One of mastery, in which he not only continued his own more original work, but — where he collaborated at all — supervised the work of less skilled dramatists, or let out certain parts of plays which he lacked time or interest to write without assistance.

(3) One in which he worked alone, or in collaboration on equal terms with other professional dramatists.

(4) The period when he was living chiefly in Stratford and may have left behind, on his visits to London, unfinished plays which he was willing to have others complete. To this period would naturally have belonged his own revisions of earlier plays, and alterations of his plays by other dramatists in London, to suit some change in public taste or some other demand. This division has the merits of greater flexibility and, on the whole, of greater probability.

There can be no wisdom in seeking to press unyielding generalisations upon Shakespeare's art and spiritual development. He himself must often have been unable to say where life left off in its influence upon his writing and art began. He was keenly alive to the dramatic fashions of his own day and followed practically all of them, without seeking to initiate any others — chronicle history, romantic comedy, tragedy of blood, pastoral, etc. Critics have found it hard to discover whether fashion or personal mood threw his tragedies into his middle years of work and such plays as *Cymbeline, The Tempest* and *The Winter's Tale* at the end. Whatever the explanation, it is true that he began his more original work with light comedy; worked forward through his more serious comedies and his slighter tragedies into the great tragedies of his third period, and ended with tragi-comedies inferior to all except his beginnings in vital power and the interpretation of life. No formula is adequate for explaining this course of development.

Shakespeare's Audiences.

The clamorous rabble which stood in the pit of the Elizabethan theatre was a formidable warning to any dramatist not to lapse for a moment into dulness. Sailors, apprentices, and many others of equally turbulent sort, standing, with the sky overhead, and the ground under foot, would not have found close attention easy, if their wills had been of the best. As it was, the conditions of attention were like those of a music hall or a circus of to-day. The audience in the pit ate nuts and apples freely, drank beer, quarrelled with actors who violated their preference, and often roared and hissed according to the effect of the play upon them. Those who sat elsewhere in the theatre brought to bear manners somewhat less noisy, but made the same insistent demand for vivid sensations.

Life was being lived at high pressure outside and had, of course, to be heightened in the theatre, in order to keep the illusions of romance or of stage emphasis. Prevalent brutalities of punishment, familiarity with death in repulsive forms, sudden reverses of fortune from court disfavour or other causes, brought it about that nothing seemed too raw or repellent to swell the excitement desired. People were receptive in imagination, credulous to a degree, and eager above all for a story interest. They had no newspapers, and the stage thus represented to them not only romance but vivid actualities as well. Yet with all its faults, an Elizabethan audience must have been far more stimulating than the average one of to-day; both because they demanded the presentation of a more vivid life and because with which they defined more freely their attitude towards what was presented. Dekker in his *Guls horn-booke* [4] gives a vivid picture of the behaviour of the Elizabethan young man of fashion at a private theatre — of his late arrival, his lavish dress, his noisy entrance upon the stage, his talk with the actors during the play, his criticism of the dramatist, and his final stalking from the theatre to express his disgust with the play.

We tend to forget in reading Shakespeare's plays, whether they are tragedies or comedies or of other kinds, that much which seems to us unconvincing to-

[4] The book should be read entire, especially, however, the chapters treating of the gallant in the playhouse, in the tavern, in the ordinary, and in Paul's Walk.

day would have passed without question then as, being within the bounds of probability or of proper romance. Certain strongly marked types, such as the villain, Don John, in *Much Ado About Nothing,* or even *Richard III,* fitted more naturally into people's understanding and experience when a sovereign was exercising full right over the life and death of her subjects, and the air was full of intrigues of every kind. Life was more a game of hazard than now, personalities came out more sharply, and, as a rule, played their parts much more swiftly. Moreover, self-repression was not esteemed the virtue it is held to be to-day, so that personal characteristics tended more naturally to excess. On the other hand, we often take even such Elizabethan types as these cited too seriously. Ford, the jealous husband in *The Merry Wives of Windsor,* expressed his jealousy in a more melodramatic way than most husbands in similar situations to-day might take. He would, to be sure, have been an absurd figure to Elizabethans as he is to us; but absurd to them for the very reason that he was not impossible from their own point of view. To us the absurdity comes largely from his being unconvincing.

VI

ACTORS CONTEMPORARY WITH SHAKESPEARE

ENGLISH dramatic companies of the professional sort began very informally, chiefly as servants of the nobility seeking to provide entertainment for their masters and, in the intervals, travelling about the country to gain further remuneration by their performances. By Shakespeare's time the profession of acting had developed sufficiently for them to form independent organisations, seeking the protection of the nobility because of certain legal and financial advantages. A company usually represented the combination of about half a score of important actors, who divided the authority and the gains, employing minor actors and other underlings for a stated sum. The more important companies associated themselves with certain theatrical managements or groups of theatres; the Burbages, father and sons, representing one such theatrical management; and Philip Henslowe and his son-in-law, Edward Alleyn, another. One company, under various names according to its patron, was identified with the Burbage management and financial returns, becoming in time the dominant theatrical influence in London. Shakespeare was, from the beginning to the end of his career, associated with this one company and its group of theatres. Henslowe's management involved a more mixed and shifting constituency of companies.

When James Burbage, father of the famous actor Richard, was in control of Shakespeare's company, it was first known as the Earl of Leicester's men; then, as Lord Strange's men, the Earl of Derby's, Lord Hunsdon's, etc., according to the title of the patron. Later in Elizabeth's reign the elevation of Lord Hunsdon to the post of Lord Chamberlain made them known as the Lord Chamberlain's men, and immediately on the accession of James I they became the King's company, retaining that title until long after Shakespeare's death. Richard Burbage was the great actor of the company in all the time of Shakespeare's connection with it, and Edward Alleyn the leading one associated permanently with Henslowe. William Kemp was for most of his career the leading comedian with Burbage, but seems to have left him for a short time about the year 1600 to play in Henslowe's company. Good acting was probably much more evenly distributed through a company than it is to-day. The permanent organisation of companies was of great practical advantage to the companies themselves, to the individual actors, and to the dramatists who provided plays for them. Certain traditions of acting could be steadily developed, and a dramatist knew the actor for whom he was writing a part. This last fact might have proved a limitation in lesser hands

than those of Burbage and Shakespeare; but it seems
never to have interfered with the complexity of Shakespeare's individual characters, or with his differentia-
tion of the many rôles written for a single actor. It
is likely that all his more important serious rôles were
written for Burbage, and that the two kept fairly even
pace in the development of their artistic powers —
Shakespeare in conceiving these characters and Burbage in presenting them.

The Calling of an Actor.

At the beginning of Elizabeth's reign the actor's
status both before the law and in social life was highly
unfortunate, as the rougher, more lawless sort had
brought great discredit upon the profession. The
Elizabethan law protecting those under the patronages
of the nobility removed this disability to some extent,
but not entirely; but the fact that the actor was " in
the statutes "—i.e., subject to legal supervision and
penalties in his calling — branded him and gave his
enemies a ready weapon against him. The very patronage which saved the actor from the law brought
with it a suggestion of servility. There was much opposition to endure from the Puritans, too; and indeed
much cause for such opposition. Shakespeare seems
to express a certain sense of the degradation of his
calling when he speaks in his sonnets of his name as
having received " a brand," or his being " in disgrace with fortune and men's eyes," etc.

On the other hand the devotion of the age to the

theatre gave the good actor an easy road to fortune. A university play of the time calls acting " the most excellent vocation in the world for money," declaring that men " come from north and south " to bring it to the playhouse of Burbage and Shakespeare. The same play describes actors as riding through the streets in satin suits with pages to attend them; and we know by the wills of various actors that they had accumulated many of the possessions associated with wealth. Also, it was possible for more than one to rise far enough above the social odium attached to his calling to acquire a coat-of-arms and to enjoy the distinction of being called *Mr.* Shakespeare and Burbage both had these rewards of their success.

Travelling Actors.

As a rule the best London companies, such as Shakespeare's, stayed within the city for their performances; but when pestilence or court displeasure, or any other cause, closed their theatres, they betook themselves to the country. Shakespeare's company seems to have travelled once because the temporary popularity of the Children of the Chapel at Blackfriars' drove them to seek patronages outside of the city. There are records of their having visited many of the towns of England.

Travelling was no easy task at best. In the more prosperous companies each actor may have provided himself with a horse, but the average player probably travelled on foot with his pack on his back, and with

the properties and boys of the company heaped together in one wagon.   That is a sad picture of Ben
Jonson, which one of his enemies recalls: " Thou
hast forgot how thou amblest by a play-wagon in the
highway to get service among the mimicks "; and that
other, of the actor toiling painfully along with his
pumps full of gravel.

Child Companies.

There were in London, besides the adult companies,
an increasing number of groups of child actors, who
were at least semi-professional in their work.   Schoolmasters first encouraged their pupils to give Latin
plays at school, as a part of their educational training;
then they devised English plays on the classical models
for them to act; and finally they widened their scope
to include plays of the miscellaneous sort presented by
the children both at court and in the city.   Another
source for child actors were the choirs of the Queen's
chapels at Whitehall and Windsor; for the children
taken at first merely to sing, came in time to con-
tribute to the Queen's pleasure by acting as well, and
those in London, known as the Children of the Chapel,
became so proficient in their art that she gave them
a private theatre, and encouraged them in every way.
A large proportion of the best dramatists of the age —
Shakespeare being a notable exception — wrote plays
for them, and some of the children became distinguished.   Salathiel Pavey, who acted the parts of old
men and for whose early death " death's self was

sorry," won very high praise from Ben Jonson; others are known to have passed from the company of the Children of the Chapel into Shakespeare's company. The experiences which went with their success could not have been very fortunate for young children, however; one gets very unprepossessing suggestions — as from the *Induction* to *Cynthia's Revels* by Ben Jonson, and from Shakespeare's allusion in *Hamlet* — of the pertness and shrewd worldliness of the Children of the Chapel. Dramatists traded on their youth to make them say what adults would not have dared, and they came under royal disfavour more than once. King James was less interested in them than Elizabeth had been, and although their company had a certain continuance in that of the Queen's Revels, their chief era was over early in the reign of James I.

It is interesting to note the many companies of school children and choir children who performed at court for the Queen, the plays which were written especially for them, and the effect upon dramatists like Lyly and Ben Jonson of writing so much for child actors. Never before or since have children been so important in the acting profession.

Shakespeare's Fellow-Actors.

The first folio edition of Shakespeare's works, published in 1623, names a long list of the principal actors in Shakespeare's plays, all associated with Shakespeare's company when they were taking parts in his plays. Many of these, however, came into the company after Shakespeare had ceased to act, and so, may not have had any close personal association with him. The more important ones with whom his name seems most directly associated are Burbage, Kemp, Pope, Phillips, Heminge, Condell, Lowin, Sly, and Armin. Among these, Burbage and Kemp are by far the most famous, although Pope and Armin were popular comedians, and Heminge and Condell were high in the counsels of the company. The last two became the editors of the first collective edition of Shakespeare's plays.

Richard Burbage.[1]

In one of Ben Jonson's plays a visitor to a puppet show asks the exhibitor which puppet is his Burbage, meaning his best player. Burbage was evidently what would be called to-day " an actor of the old school." Shakespeare's sonorous blank verse, with its long rhetorical passages, must have pleased him, for the intimate friendship, which held to the end between the two, argues very harmonious professional relations between the player and his *play-maker*.[2] Everything points to the conclusion that Burbage played such parts as those of Richard III, Othello, Lear, Macbeth, Hamlet, etc. ; and he thus becomes for Shakespeare the most important figure in his theatrical world, the one on whom he was most dependent for interpreting his plays to the public. Burbage had, like Joseph Jefferson in

[1] Portrait facing p. 96.

[2] The designation of dramatists as *play-makers* is a common one in Elizabethan documents, legal and otherwise.

modern times, much reputation for skill in painting, and evidently accumulated a comfortable fortune, besides securing the worldly satisfaction to be had from a coat-of-arms. He must have been not only an artist of very high quality, but a man of fair dealing, shrewd business sense, and capacity for lasting friendship. All that we know of him wins admiration.

William Kemp.

Kemp is one of the many picturesque figures of Elizabeth's time, and his light-hearted attitude towards life could not have been merely a matter of acting. Richard Tarleton, who was probably still playing when Shakespeare went up to London, was the great comedian up to his death in 1588, and Kemp succeeded almost at once to his place and reputation, the tradition being that Tarleton had left his spirit behind him for Kemp.   The individuality of Kemp comes out in his feats accessory to acting — as, for example, in his ability to play the tabor and pipe and dance at the same time; or in his gift of comic improvisation, which Shakespeare is thought to have censured in a passage in *Hamlet*. He was very ingenious too in devising for himself activities which would advertise him widely by their sensational character, besides promoting diversion for others.   His *Nine Daies Wonder* gives an account of a dance which he performed from London to Norwich, where the mayor welcomed him with a triumphal entry, and gave him a pension of 40 shillings.   He travelled in Italy, visiting, among other places, Venice and Rome, and is said to have danced all the way across the Alps.   Thomas Nashe tells how a celebrated Italian clown embraced him when told that he knew William Kemp, declaring that Kemp was the greatest of all clowns in the world.   He had the original rôles of Dogberry in *Much Ado About Nothing,* and of Peter in *Romeo and Juliet,* and is thought to have played one of the grave diggers in *Hamlet,* one of the Dromios in *The Comedy of Errors,* Touchstone

72. KEMP DANCING.

in *As You Like It,* etc.   It has been noted that this type of clown disappeared from Shakespeare's plays soon after Kemp left the King's company for a time; it has been surmised that Shakeseare wrote them with him especially in mind.

Shakespeare as Actor.

Shakespeare himself was probably never very successful as an actor, although he could not have been a failure, because he played at court somewhat early in his career, and praise of his acting has come down to us from his own day. The praise was well tempered, however, and he is never singled out of the company, as Burbage and Kemp so often are, for special commendation of their ability. His name appears prominently more than once in lists of actors in his company, but his success as a dramatist and his evident capacity for business would probably have kept him to the front in his company, whether he attained any real distinction as an actor or not.

Tradition.

He is said by tradition to have played the ghost in *Hamlet* and the decrepit old Adam in *As You Like It;* also to have been accustomed to playing the rôles of old men. If this is true, he had small scope for special gifts in acting, and could hardly have possessed them. Physical limitations of one sort and another have been conjectured as keeping him from pre-eminence in the profession, but nothing can be said on this point with any certainty.

VII

THEATRES

IF Shakespeare went up to London in 1586 he found only two public playhouses in existence,[1] one of them called the Theatre, because it had been for a time the only one; and the other, the Curtain.   Both were under the management of James Burbage, who belonged to the Earl of Leicester's players, later known as the Lord Chamberlain's players.   Burbage, with the easy adaptability of the Elizabethan, combined the activities of innkeeper, liveryman and actor with those of theatrical manager; and he probably knew how to dovetail them together in a way which made each of them helpful to the others.   He built the Theatre in 1576, the year after the edict forbidding the erection of playhouses within the city limits had been passed; and he chose for its site the pleasure grounds to the north of the city, away from the river.   The Curtain was erected near it in the following year.   More than twenty years later the sons of Burbage, having now succeeded him in authority, quarrelled with the owner of the ground on which the Theatre was built, and de-

---

[1] There have lately come to light documents which seem to prove that the private theatre, the Blackfriars, may have been open at this time.

cided to tear it down and rebuild it on the opposite side
of the river, in the section known as the Bankside.

73. VISSCHER'S VIEW OF LONDON, A.D. 1616.
Showing the Bear Garden and The Globe.

This they did, calling the new theatre the Globe.   It
was destroyed by fire in 1613, but immediately rebuilt

under the same name.   Before this, however, the Burbage management had secured possession of the private
theatre building known as the Blackfriars, and leased
it to the Children of the Chapel; but in 1608 they took

74.   THE GLOBE THEATRE.

it over for their own use in winter, keeping the Globe
as a summer theatre.   Blackfriars was free from the
city laws because of its origin as a monastic building.
Shakespeare's company was as well equipped as possible, when it was provided with a summer playhouse

in the favourite suburban pleasure grounds, and a winter one in the fashionable part of the city. It is with the first Globe and the Blackfriars that the earliest production of Shakespeare's greatest plays is associated, although at least twelve of them had already been acted before the first Globe was built. These were all given first either at the Theatre or at the Curtain.

It must have been very close to the time of the dramatist's arrival in London that Philip Henslowe, "wool dealer, dyer, owner of a starch factory, real estate dealer, innkeeper, pawnbroker, vestryman and churchwarden," [2] decided, in 1587, to set up a playhouse in rivalry of those owned by the Burbages in the northern fields. He chose the southern pleasure grounds for his location, and on the Bankside built for himself a theatre called the Rose. A few years later, the Swan, a playhouse in which he had an interest, was built near the Rose, to the west. It is evident that he had chosen his site wisely, for hundreds of boats plied back and forth to the city, and bear-baitings, cock-fightings, etc., were already drawing the people there in throngs. It is, therefore, not surprising that when the Burbages were at odds with their landlord, they welcomed the opportunity for separating their two theatres, and placing one at a point where they could divide with Henslowe the patronage which he was accumulating. Henslowe made a counter-move by setting up another playhouse, the Fortune, on the city side, in the direction of the Burbages' Curtain

[2] Quoted from Schelling's *Elizabethan Drama.*

75. THE SWAN THEATRE, BANKSIDE.

76. THE ROSE THEATRE.

theatre; and, later on, he built still another on the Bankside and called it the Hope.   He was fortunate in having Philip Alleyn as his son-in-law and star actor; and the combination of Alleyn's gifts as an actor with Henslowe's shrewd business sense made them very formidable competitors with Shakespeare's company

77.   THE SECOND FORTUNE PLAY-HOUSE.

for public favour; but they had no Shakespeare to provide them with plays, and Burbage was, after all, higher in popularity than Alleyn.   When King James put the seal of his favour on Shakespeare's company by adopting them as his own, the fortunes of Henslowe's theatres fell into permanent shadow.

78. QUEEN ELIZABETH'S FREE GRAMMAR SCHOOL AT ST.
SAVIOUR'S, SOUTHWARK.

79. MEDAL GRANTED TO THE BEST BOY.

80. THE STAGE USED FOR ELIZABETHAN REVIVALS AT HARVARD.

81. THE YARD OF "THE FOUR SWANS."
A typical Elizabethan Inn.

Performances.

The openness of the public theatres to the sky made them dependent on fair weather, and all performances were announced subject to this. In London they took place every day except Sunday, and were in the afternoon. They were supposed to be ended before darkness came on, beginning about three o'clock, and lasting for two hours or more. Playbills were posted about the city, by some theatres, if not by all, and a flag on the building gave local sign of an intended play. The beginning of the performance was announced by three blasts of a trumpet, and immediately afterwards the prologue appeared on the stage to entreat the favour of the audience for the play. At the public theatres the price for admission began at one penny and reached as much as a half crown,[3] the pit being unprovided with seats except for those who were willing to pay an extra sixpence for a stool. At Blackfriars the more expensive seats cost as much as eight shillings.

Structure of the Theatres.
Public Theatres.

The structure of the first public theatres is largely explained by the places where plays were given before any theatres were built. These places were the innyards, the courtyards of castles and the amphitheatres or rings designed for the baiting of animals. In the old innyards the conditions had been very simple and

[3] 2s 6d, or about sixty-two cents.

yet very practical both for actors and for audience. The religious plays had been given on wagons drawn into the court or yard with the actors upon them, and the rabble had massed themselves in front of these wagons, standing on the ground or sitting on stools or benches to watch the play, while the more fortunate looked down from the balconies or windows surrounding the yard. Most of the public theatres adopted all of these features, modifying and supplementing them as necessity required. The playhouse was uncovered in the centre and covered on the sides in a way which corresponded to the yard and balconies of the old inns. The covered part included in some theatres a portion of the stage which projected far out into the open space known as the pit. The stage was open on all sides except at the back, where dressing rooms, called tiring rooms, were built on. In some of the playhouses a change was made from both the square and the circular shape to the polygonal, the many angles affording a better view for spectators at a distance from the stage.

Stages of Public Theatres.

Some Elizabethan theatres were used alternately for bear-baitings and for dramatic performances, so that they naturally made use of the movable stage which must disappear when the bear-baitings were to occur. Permanent stages had coverings which extended forward to about the middle and were supported by pillars.

The main stage of most public theatres could itself be considered as three stages — the outer one beyond

82. INTERIOR OF THE OLD SWAN THEATRE.

the pillars; the middle one, reaching from the pillars back to the part under the balcony; and the inner one, which was under the balcony. The outer and middle

stages might serve together in a play to represent a
city, or street, or field; and the inner one, under the balcony, as a house, or room, or cave, or cell; or the plan
might be reversed, and the back of the stage be considered the entrance, with the outer and middle stages
together as an interior; or still other adjustments could,
of course, be made. High up over the back was a
" heavens," where properties were stored and let down
upon the stage. The heavens served, too, as a place
from which supernatural characters in the play could
descend, and to which they could be drawn up. An
under-stage served as the abode of ghosts, evil spirits,
etc.; and there was a balcony over the back of the main
stage to be used as an upper stage.[4]

Stage Curtains.

There could have been in the public theatres no curtain for the unroofed, outer stage, because there was
no way of fastening it from above or at the sides. It
is almost as difficult to conceive of a middle curtain
hung from the pillars supporting the heavens, because
on a projecting stage, with the seats running along the
sides to the back, there would have been little stage
privacy behind this front curtain, unless side curtains
connecting with it had also been arranged, and this
would have been awkward in appearance and in opera-

[4] The picture here given of the interior of the Swan theatre
is not authentic in all details but illustrates better than any
other extant illustration the projecting stage, the large balcony
at the back, the heavens, the balconies for the audience, and the
supporting stage pillars.

tion.　This middle curtain would also have shut off the
balcony in all scenes where the inner stage was hidden.
There was probably no curtain at all except that for
the inner stage and for the balcony over it; and it seems

83. STAGE OF THE RED BULL THEATRE.

reasonable to suppose that this curtain was in two sections, so that either of these stages could be used or
hidden without involving the other.[5]　One of the most

[5] The date of this picture is 1672 and it is, like that of the Swan
theatre, not reliable in all respects, but is useful as showing the
balcony over the rear stage as well as the divided curtains.

interesting reconstructions of the Elizabethan public stage is the one made by Professor George P. Baker of Harvard University for revivals of Elizabethan plays, although this does not show a divided curtain at the back.

84. INTERIOR OF GRAY'S INN HALL.

Blackfriars.

The structure of the Blackfriars theatre, the only important private playhouse during most of Shakespeare's residence in London, grew mainly out of its having been at first a monastic building. It was square in shape and was naturally roofed over; its stage did not project out into the pit but ran directly across the whole width of the hall, which had been made by knocking out the walls between several rooms. The smallness of the house, as compared with the size of the public theatres, carried a suggestion of exclusiveness, and this was accentuated by the high cost of admission. Perhaps the night performance, the privilege of sitting on the stage, and the Queen's connection with the management while the Children of the Chapel were there, tended also to win popularity for it. Other private theatres — Whitefriars, the Cockpit, and Salisbury Court — imitated all the imitable features of Blackfriars, but none of them attained the same distinction or popularity.

Scenery.

Scenery was certainly used to some extent at court performances, and one of the child actors at Blackfriars talks of being himself taken as " a piece of perspective," as though scenery with perspective were an accepted feature of the stage. Later on, in an Oxford play given to entertain royalty, the scene was changed three times, although we have an incomplete idea of what these changes involved. On the public stage, however, there was apparently very little, if any, of what is known to-day as scenery; and the very lack of effort to provide a suitable background tended to multiply changes of scene in a play, just as the elaborate requirements for setting a scene realistically to-day make it a point of dramatic technique for the scene to be changed as seldom as possible. Signs were sometimes hung on the stage to indicate a locality, and sometimes two signs remained in sight throughout a performance, to indicate that both places were involved. Sir Philip Sidney alludes contemptuously to the custom of signs on the stage when he asks: " What child will believe that a place is Thebes because the word ' Thebes ' is written in great letters upon an old door? " but it is probable that this custom of locality signs did not last in good theatres through the Elizabethan age, and that it was never universal. Sidney also suggests the extravagant demand made upon the spectator's imagination by declaring that Asia may be expected on one side of the stage and Africa on the other; but he indicates a second way in which scenes were placed for the spectator, by saying that the players begin immediately on their entrance to explain where the action is to take place. This means, of course, that the dramatist puts the explanation into the dialogue.

Actors did extemporise at times, especially in low comedy parts, but such explanations as these would come characteristically from the author.

Properties.

There were probably more properties on the Elizabethan stage than Ben Greet and some others attempting revivals of Elizabethan conditions have been willing to allow. The general conception of stage setting which obtained then as regards properties was undoubtedly crude enough, however, and Sidney also attacked this conception in a passage as famous as the two just mentioned:

"Now ye shall have three ladies walk to gather flowers and then we must believe the stage to be a garden. By and by we hear news of a shipwreck in the same place, and then we are to blame if we accept it not for a rock. Upon the back of that comes out a hideous monster with fire and smoke, and then the miserable beholders are bound to take it for a cave. While in the meantime two armies fly in, represented with four swords and bucklers, and then what hard heart will not receive it for a pitched field?"

Some set piece of green was probably a usual part of the stage equipment, serving indifferently to represent a tree, a forest, etc. So a bed would suggest a chamber; a throne, a palace; a steeple, a church; etc.; and entirely mismatched properties probably often stood together on the stage throughout a play, each to serve its turn when needed. The principle was, of course, the same as that which permitted the two signs of locality on the stage at once. Some of the properties must have been very troublesome to devise; as, for example, the one in *Friar Bacon and Friar Bungay,* where Bungay conjures out of the ground a tree " with a fire-

shooting dragon " similar to the one which Sidney rid-
icules; or another in *All for Money,* where the stage
directions order Pleasure to appear from beneath
" with some fine conveyance."

What the stage artist evidently attempted, if such
a special functionary existed, was symbolic suggestion rather than full or realistic representation. He
counted, too, upon the dramatist to indicate difficult
scenes, and to give enough descriptions within the dialogue to cover most of the necessities of stage setting;
but both the dramatist and the stage artist trusted
vastly more to the imagination of the audience than
either would dare to do to-day.

Heavy properties such as beds, may have been kept
on the inner stage, which could be shut off from the
others by a curtain hung below the balcony.   Sometimes the old stage directions seem to indicate that a
bed was pushed forward from behind at a certain point
in a play; but it is probable that very heavy properties
like beds, thrones, battlements, etc., were usually set
on the stage in advance.

Costumes.

The comparative barrenness of the stage as regards
properties was partly obscured in the minds of the spectators by the elaborate costumes of the actors.   Contemporary writings have many allusions to the gorgeous and expensive dress of actors, even when off
the stage; and they probably took care to see that
their stage costumes were still more striking.   In the

main, the English dress of the different social orders
and types for their own day was probably used; but it
would be wrong to infer that the practice admitted of
no variations. There were many accepted conventions
of costume in the public mind, both for classical figures
and for contemporary continental nations; and a people
as busy with contemporary foreign fashions in their
own dress could not have been tolerant of the actors'
complete ignoring of these fashions. Nor is it likely
that, in a city abounding in foreigners whose national
fashions of dress were familiar to all, actors would
have made no attempt to reproduce these fashions when
the characters involved made them appropriate. Foreign fashions indeed would inevitably have appeared
in the actual Elizabethan costumes. In *Love's Labour's Lost* the King and his train disguise themselves
in Russian garments; and court records have many
items of expense for costumes for such characters as
Turks, patriarchs, etc., with descriptions of dress very
different from that of the prevailing English fashion.
Gods and goddesses, dragons, devils, and various other
characters, brought over from the religious plays and
the masques, required costumes not of any usual English sort. We need to remember that the Elizabethans
— Shakespeare, his fellow dramatists, fellow actors
and their audiences all alike — cared little for close
historical exactness in costume, setting or even in the
foreign life and spirit represented; and yet we tend
to underestimate the intelligence of the Elizabethans
at some points and to overestimate it at others. But

whatever may have been the equipment of the Elizabethan stage, it was a challenge to the imagination of the dramatist and to that of the actor and of the audience as well.

VIII

JAMES THE FIRST AS A PATRON OF THE DRAMA

MENTION has already been made of the custom of historians of dramatic literature to include as Elizabethan all drama from the accession of Elizabeth in 1558, through the reigns of James I and Charles I to the closing of the theatres in 1642 at the beginning of Cromwell's administration. The custom rests on the realisation that one creative impulse, rising to a climax and then declining into almost complete decay, was at work through all this time, and that Elizabeth and her reign gave it the real impetus and vitality. The earlier glory lingered on for a time in the work of many Jacobeans, but the decline set in very soon after the accession of James in 1603.

There were, indeed, several reasons why the reign of James I was especially auspicious for the drama. Although personally far less energising as a patron than Queen Elizabeth, he was almost as conspicuous a devotee of the drama, and fostered it in a thoroughly practical way from the beginning of his reign. Several of the well-known theatres were built in his reign, and his distribution, almost immediately on his accession, of the important companies of actors among the

different members of the royal family, as their servants
to be especially befriended, is an illustration of the constructive interest which he took in the prosperity of
the drama, although he had undoubtedly some reasons
of state for this policy.   He encouraged both public
and private theatres, and at court pushed the masque
to the highest development it has ever attained, with
Ben Jonson as their chief writer and Inigo Jones as
stage architect and artist.   The expense of some of
the masques presented before King James seems fab-
ulous even to us, with our standard of sumptuous
stage spectacle; and some of the intricate devices used
would do credit to the best scientific skill at work in
modern staging.

Still another reason why the reign of James I was
favourable to the drama lay in the advance which had
been made by this time in the understanding of dramatic technique.   It has already been pointed out that
when Elizabeth came to the throne would-be dramatists
had only the crudest conceptions of what might con-
stitute a play — story, spectacle, interlude, triumph,
etc., mingling indiscriminately under that name.   At
the close of her reign, there was still ample indiffer-
ence to classical requirements, but the art of plot making, or of conceiving and dealing with situation, had
developed enormously, and characterisation had taken
on sustained power and intensity in the hands of many
dramatic writers.   Jonson, as the champion of classical niceties, had explained and illustrated his careful
theories; and Shakespeare was winning his great tri-

85. MARY, QUEEN OF SCOTS.

86. KING JAMES I.

From a painting by P. van Somer, dated 1621, in the
National Portrait Gallery.

umphs in technique by daring to violate most of the stricter injunctions which Jonson laid down. Many lesser dramatists of real power had also become conscious of practical principles underlying successful dramatic construction. Beaumont and Fletcher, beginning to write early in the reign of King James, were vastly richer in teachers and models than even Shakespeare had been, although it was late in the reign of Elizabeth when he began his activity. In pure stagecraft and technique, according to the taste of their times, Beaumont and Fletcher have perhaps never been surpassed in England; for they understood every art needed for pleasing their public, and they worked without waste in securing their effects: everything in their plays told for immediate effect. The Jacobean dramatists had much for which to be grateful.

But in a deeper sense the Jacobean drama, fortunate in so many ways, inherited from the Elizabethan drama the seeds of its own decay. All the full flood of enthusiasm which had surged in the spirit of Elizabethan England expressed itself in the drama of that time; and the enthusiasm had spent itself with the extravagance of achievement and emotion. The spirit of England was no longer young and expectant; and, as dramatic art advanced, the sources of dramatic inspiration tended towards decline. The stirring times came somehow to seem ended, all great adventures to have been tried. The era of the really romantic drama had passed, and a drama which piled one artificiality upon another came to take its place, aiming at a succession of sharp surprises and violent contrasts. The moral tone of the drama, sickened, too, sometimes into a fetid affectation of morality; sometimes into an open love of the lewd. These undermining influences left untouched many of the better dramatists of the time; but the taint was there, and it is seen very markedly in Fletcher. From him and others the infection spread until it culminated in the morbid fantasies of Ford.

Shakespeare was, of course, no victim to these signs of decay. He followed the fashions of the times in the types of drama which he used, and in points of literary style he fell into more than one of the minor literary faults of his time — euphuism, verbal quibbling, etc.; but his large firm grasp of life kept him sound in his presentation of its serious issues, and his poetic genius saved him from lapsing into any grievous literary sins.

Shakespeare's own relation to James I and his court must have been a very friendly one, although it must inevitably have lacked such inspiration as Elizabeth's reign had furnished him. It was probably Shakespeare's prestige among playwrights, as well as Burbage's among actors, which made the King choose their company to be called his own servants; Shakespeare is named second in the list of actors then mentioned as granted by the King, the right " freely to use and exercise the arte and faculty of playing comedies, tragedies, histories, interludes, moralls, pastorals, stage-plaies, and such other like as they have already studied or hereafter shall use or studie, as well for the

recreation of our lovinge subjects, as for our solace
and pleasure when we shall thinke good to see them,
duringe our pleasure." His name appears first too in
the list of actors in the procession for James's entry
into London in the following year, and we know that he
was one of the nine from the King's company which
wore on that occasion the King's scarlet livery for
which cloth was granted them. There are records that
Shakespeare's company appeared at least a dozen times
before the King, and of their receiving thirty pounds
once when they played before him at Wilton in the Earl
of Pembroke's house. Whether Shakespeare himself
ever acted at court after James's accession, we do not
know. There is no record at all of his acting after the
year of James's accession, and there were several years
before his death when his residence in Stratford would
itself have made his appearance in a court performance
seem improbable. It seems likely, however, that if,
in the first years of James's reign, Shakespeare was
still acting, he appeared in some of the plays which
his company gave before the Kings.

IX

ELIZABETHAN MUSIC

The Queen's Love of Music.

THE twelve trumpets and pair of drums which "made the hall ring for a half hour together" at Greenwich before the Queen's dinner, are only one of the many signs of her fondness for music, which was apparently second only to that for the drama. The records of her household show that it included at one time twelve trumpeters, six sackbut players, three drummers, two flute players, two lute players, one rebeck player, eight violinists, two harpists, two players on the virginal, two makers of instruments, eight adult singers, six "singing children," nine minstrels and seven "musician strangers." There were probably many occasions when this household force was greatly augmented. The Queen was herself a skilled player on the virginal, and Lord Melville, one of the nobility of her time, has left this story of his coming upon her once while she was playing upon it:

"The same day after dinner, my Lord of Hunsdean [Hunsdon] drew me up to a quiet gallery that I might hear some music (but he said he durst not avow it), where I might hear the Queen play upon the virginals. After I had hearkened a while I took by the tapestry that hung before the door of the chamber, and seeing her back was towards the door, I entered within the chamber and stood a pretty space, hearing her play excellently well; but she left off immediately so soon as she turned her about, and came forward, seeming to strike me with her hand, alledging she was not used to play before men, but when she was solitary, to shun melancholy."

A less alluring but amusing picture of the Queen's interest in music is found in the story of her disputes with Dr. Tye, one of the famous musicians associated with the Chapel Royal.

" Dr. Tye was a peevish and humorous man, especially in his latter days; and sometimes playing on the organ in the Chapel of Queen Elizabeth, what contained much music, but little delight to the ear, she would send the verger to tell him that he played out of tune: whereupon he sent word to her that her ears were out of tune."

The musical features of many of the entertainments tendered her on her progresses, whether dialogues, triumphs, or of other sort, is another proof of her fondness for music. At Kenilworth very soon after her arrival, musicians for personal attendance upon her were presented her by her host, to serve her at her pleasure during her long stay; and at Elvetham the famous pageant on the pond achieved very beautiful artistic effects with the musicians in one boat answering those of another with lutes and cornets, etc. Nor did the Queen trust her musical entertainment entirely to the generous provisions of her hosts when she visited among her subjects; for six of the Gentlemen of the Chapel and six of the Children were a part of her appointed retinue on such occasions.

The Children of the Chapel.

The Children of the Chapel, in time so famous as actors, were chosen primarily for their ability to sing, and the Queen gave to her London choir-master the same right to take possession of children whose voices were likely to please her, as she gave to the Master of the Revels to command all resources for her dramatic entertainment. More than once a parent's natural affection and anger were aroused to protest by having his boy taken from him with the prospect of several years' absence in the Queen's service; but she made some amends for this form of self-indulgence by maintaining the children comfortably, and by providing for them education, both in academic studies and in the arts. A German duke who visited Blackfriars theatre during the time when the Children of the Chapel were giving dramatic performances there, tells how the children were " required to devote themselves earnestly to the art of singing and to learn to play on various sorts of musical instruments," having teachers to instruct them in all the arts, but the most excellent of all in music. He adds this description of the children's concert at the theatre:

"For a whole hour preceding the play, one listens to delightful musical entertainment on organs, lutes, pandomis, mandolins, violins and flutes, as on the present occasion, when a boy *cum voce tremula* sang so charmingly to the accompaniment of a bass-viol that unless possibly the nuns at Milan may have excelled him, we had not heard his equal on our journey."

Noted Elizabethan Musicians.

The Chapel Royal had been, from the time of Henry the Eighth, the centre for the best musical talent of England, and besides the Children and Gentlemen of the Chapel, most of the celebrated musicians of Elizabeth's time were, in one way or another, connected with it. Music, both as a science and as an art, made rapid advance in Elizabeth's reign. Musical composition, orchestration of the simpler sort, sight singing and part singing, the making of musical instruments, etc., all shared in the development. There were many noted composers, among whom the chief were Dr. Bull, William Byrd, Orlando Gibbons, Giles Farnaby, Thomas Morley, and John Dowland — all players upon some instrument at court and in the houses of the nobility. They wrote the music for many of the Elizabethan songs and published many collections of songs. Gibbons's *Madrigals and Metres for Five Voices* and *Fantasies in Three Parts;* Morley's *First Set of Ballets,* and his *Plain and Easy Introduction to Practical Music;* Byrd's *Psalmes, Sonets, and Songs;* Dowland's *First Set of Songs,* etc., are only suggestive of the vast number which appeared.

The whole age was musical. The Queen set the fashion, but for many reasons it was the time for England to sing, and music of all kinds abounded. The hearty English countryman had always had his songs and still has them; but never before or since have Englishmen of the higher classes so flung away their reserve and yielded to the call of song. Music swept like a wave over the city, the court, and the houses of the nobility, as a natural expression of the spirit of the time. The instruments which are set down in an inventory of the possessions of a noble house in Suffolk in 1602 show a zeal for music rivalling even that of the Queen:

" Six viols, six violins, seven recorders, six cornets, one mute cornet, four lutes, a bandore, a cittern, two sack-buts, three haut-boys, a bassoon, two flutes, two small virginals, two double virginals, a wind instrument like a virginall, two large organs."

Besides this list of instruments, there are mentioned in the inventory two " lewting books," many song books, and fifteen books of dance music to be played upon several instruments in concert.

The spread of the fashion of music was greatly furthered by the emphasis upon it as a necessary part of the education of both sexes, especially among those who aspired to any gentility. William Byrd in his *Psalmes, Sonets, and Songs,* published in 1583, gives a succession of urgent reasons why every one should learn to sing. Singing, he declares, is easily taught and quickly learned; it is " delightful to nature " and a preservative of health; it strengthens all parts of the breast and opens the pipes; it is a singularly good remedy for stuttering and stammering; it is the best of all means to secure a perfect pronunciation and make a good public speaker; it is the only way to discover a natural gift for song; it offers a musical pleasure to which that derived from no instrument is comparable; it affords a means of serving God, and the voice of man is chiefly to be employed to that end. Thomas Morley, in his *Plain and Easy Introduction to Practical Music,* which was published fourteen years after Byrd's book, goes even further, implying that a man who cannot read at sight and sing one of the parts in a harmony is half a boor. He tells how, after a banquet, a company were furnished by the hostess with parts for a song, and when one of the guests declared his inability to take part, the others began to ask one another in surprise where he could have been brought up. In *The Winter's Tale* Shakespeare shows two crude country people, Dorcus and Mopsa, at a sheep shearing, starting in promptly on their parts in a song which they have just purchased from the pedlar, Autolycus — Autolycus himself taking the initial part and the song running in this succession:

Autol. Get you hence for I must go
Where it fits not you to know.
Dor. Whither? *M.* O whither? *D.* Whither?
M. It becomes thy oath full well
Thou to me thy secrets tell.
D. Me too, let me go thither.
M. Or thou goest to the grange or mill.
D. If to either, thou doest ill.

A.   Neither. *D.* What, neither? *A.* Neither.
D.   Thou hast sworn my love to be
        Thou hast sworn it more to me
        Then whither goest? Say whither?

Certain kinds of songs often became associated with special occupations, as ballads with pedlars, catches with tinkers, etc. Dekker in his *Wonderful Year* gives a very characteristic picture of a travelling tinker and his musical gifts:

"At last a tinker came sounding through the towne . . . a devout tinker he did honour God Pan; a musicall tinker that upon his kettle drums could play any country dance you cal'd for and upon Holly dayes had earned money by it when no fiddler could be heard of. He was onely feared when he stalkt through some towns where bees were, for he struck so sweetely on the bottom of his copper instrument that he would empty whole hives and lead the swarms after him only by the sound."

Carters won a special name for whistling; apprentices in various crafts had their songs. It is said that a youth seeking employment could speak with confidence of a gift for singing, as one of his assets towards pleasing a master. With the prevailing rivalry of apprentices and the popularity of music, the master doubtless felt that a musical apprentice brought a distinct advertising value. There were for actual use also, besides these songs of trades, many hunting songs, dawn songs, evening songs, tavern songs, etc. Nicholas Breton's delightful lyric, " In the merry month of May," was sung first as a dawn song under the window of Queen Elizabeth during her visit to Kenilworth.

Elizabethan songs are hard to classify, but are perhaps most conveniently considered as (1) those of native growth, and (2) those based on models from the Continent. Popular songs of one nation almost inevitably resemble those of another in a similar stage of development, but there is always a strongly indigenous quality besides.

Native Songs.

Of the native songs, the round, the catch, and the ballad were the most popular, especially among the lower classes. The example just cited of the round shows how the words assigned to each singer fell into the structure of a dialogue, but it does not make clear the structure of the music. This involves the beginning of the singers, not all at once as in most songs, but singly in a certain succession, each starting with the beginning of the tune for himself. Shakespeare's round is not a perfect succession of parts because Autolycus sings less often than the others; but very few definitions were closely applied by Elizabethans, and there were often times when this very fact was an unconscious element in their art.

This looseness of definition applies to the catch as well as the round.[1] The catch, like the round, involves

[1] The round is, by dictionary definition, "a short melody so composed as to produce harmony when sung by several voices starting at successive intervals of time."

a succession of singers, beginning one after another, and, theoretically, it requires one singer to catch up the words of another in such a way as to mispronounce both and pervert the meaning.

A classic illustration of such a process is the pronouncing of " Ah, how Sophia, etc. ! " as " A house-afire." Catches were the favourite songs over the cup, the amusement caused by the perverted meanings of words evidently offering special appeal when the sense of humour had been properly stimulated by drink. Shakespeare is fond of using the catch, and instances of its use are found in *The Taming of the Shrew, As You Like It, Twelfth Night,* and *The Tempest.*

The ballad characteristically involved, then as now, a narrative element, and was not only the most widespread musical expression among common people, but a reflection of social life — often an expression of animosity and of biting satire — a chronicle of stirring historical events, a song of romantic adventure: in brief, a mould into which any tale of life could be poured. It was a dangerous weapon in the hands of many hot-blooded Elizabethans, and had played its part in many political situations until Elizabeth silenced it there by edict.

Ballads of adventure ran any length of extravagance. Autolycus peddling his ballads in *The Winter's Tale* seems to be laughing at some of this sort.

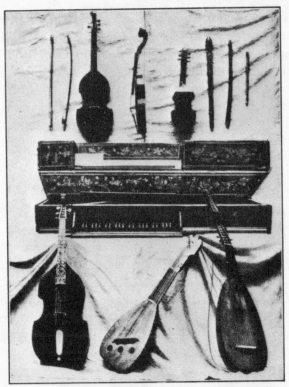

87. A GROUP OF ELIZABETHAN MUSICAL INSTRUMENTS.

88. TWO OF THE THREE AUTOGRAPH SIGNATURES,
Severally written by Shakespeare on his Will on March 25, 1616
(Reproduced from the original document now at Somerset
House, London.)

89. QUEEN ELIZABETH'S VIRGINAL.

Songs of Foreign Origin.

Songs based on continental models were of many kinds, but were chiefly madrigals and canzonets. Sonnets were also of Italian origin and were sometimes sung, but much less often than the other two. Even in Italy the madrigal was somewhat flexibly interpreted as to structure, but a definition of Elizabethan madrigals is practically impossible. Thomas Watson illustrates this in his *Italian Madrigals Englished,* where he frequently departs from both the text and the form of his Italian originals. Theoretically, however, an Italian madrigal is a short non-stanzaic poem with a definite metrical form of correspondence between certain lines.[2] The Italian canzone, from which the Elizabethan canzonet is derived, is a stanzaic poem in which each stanza conforms to a somewhat elaborate metrical structure of recurring rhyme, the lines being often of varying lengths. Most of the songs of foreign origin are in a tone of languishing lament over the lady's hardness of heart. On the whole, although the Elizabethan song-makers were vastly indebted to the Italians and to the French for help in understanding the artistry of song-making, the best songs which remain to us from that time are those which carry a certain suggestion of artlessness and are most expressive of the English spirit. Some of the most delight-

[2] The modern definition of the madrigal as: "a short amatory or pastoral poem in iambic metre," is helpful as to subjects of madrigals if the word *pastoral* may be taken to designate *poems of nature.*

ful of the Elizabethan songs were written by the dramatists for inclusion in their plays, and we are apt to read them without realising that they are only half alive unless they are sung. Delightful examples of such lyrics are in Shakespeare's and Fletcher's plays; in Peele's and Lyly's as well.

Besides the songs, there was a large amount of instrumental music in the plays, although the plays, as written down, do not always include mention of either. For one of the well-known plays of the time, record remains that between the first and second acts cornets and organs played; between the second and the third, organs with recorders; between the third and fourth, organs and viols; and between the fourth and fifth, the bass lute and treble. Some well-known poets were also composers, writing the music as well as the words for their songs. Thomas Campion was one of the most popular of this group.

Musical Instruments.

Among musical instruments the virginal was the one most distinctively appropriated by the feminine sex, probably deriving its name from its special appropriateness for young girls.[3] It was well adapted for accompanying singing, and is best compared to the piano among modern instruments, although much smaller, less varied in tone, and less rich in volume. The lute and cittern were also stringed instruments suitable for accompanying the voice, and the lute, especially, ad-

[3] For the virginal see illustration facing p. 164.

mitted of several varieties. It was highly popular and is said to have hung in the barber shops of the time, so as to furnish diversion to waiting customers. The cittern resembled a guitar but had wire strings and was played with a quill. Both lute and cittern were much used by women as well as by men. Bandores also were like the guitar, and were used to furnish the base to the cittern. Rebecks were three stringed instruments played with a bow. There were also many kinds of viols or violins, including the viol da gamba, which was nearest to the 'cello of to-day. Among wind instruments there was much development in Shakespeare's time, many new ones being added in the sixteenth century. Sackbuts, more or less comparable to the modern trombone, were much in favour; hautboys, known also as shawms or waits, are mentioned in the stage directions of many Elizabethan plays, and were popular for music at banquets; they were seven-holed wooden tubes providing treble for a bassoon. Recorders were really flutes, having seven holes and a whistle at the mouth; they, too, are often named as used in plays. Cornets and fifes were made of wood, but were wind instruments as now. The fife was a small, six-holed instrument somewhat like a flute, but giving out a sound resembling that of whistling; it suggests the recorder in this, but is much less dignified in its associations. The bassoon was a wooden wind instrument used to furnish the bass for the oboe.

Large drums, sometimes called tabourines, belonged

to imposing occasions — war, funeral processions, etc. Timbrels were smaller and, unlike the drum, were covered only at one end of the round wooden frame, somewhat as the tambourine of the Spanish dancer is to-day, although more hollow, and meant to give out its sound by being struck. The tabor was also a small drum to be struck, but was covered at both ends, and its wooden frame was often much deeper in proportion to the diameter than it is in the modern drum. It could be struck with the hand as well as with a stick; and, especially in combination with the pipe, was much loved of the common people — the pipe furnishing most of the melody and the tabor the very cheerful and dance-provoking noise.

Elizabethan trumpets, like drums, were for large occasions at court,— war, royal processions, welcomes to royalty, etc. They were very long, and are said to have somewhat resembled bugles in their sound. It will be remembered that when Queen Elizabeth visited Kenilworth, trumpeters blew their welcome to her from silver trumpets five feet long. A *consort* was an Elizabethan concert of instrumental music rendered by a number of instruments. A *whole* consort was performed on instruments all of the same sort, e.g. lutes, recorders, etc. A *broken* consort included instruments of different kinds playing in harmony — as viols, lutes, cornets, etc.

The astonishing musical development in Elizabethan England did not bear the permanent fruit which might have been expected of the English as a nation. The

era remains one of the great landmarks in the history
of music, however, because of the advance made in the
development of musical instruments and of musical
composition. The close connection of music and the
dance, and the necessity for writing music suitable for
sequences of dances, is said to have had a marked effect in paving the way for the modern suite and sonata.
Other music of the time is said to have anticipated the
fugue.[4] This in itself is a striking contribution to artistic progress, and certainly the large body of Elizabethan songs which have come down to us instinct with
life and melody is of no less value either to music or
to literature.

Shakespeare's Interest in Music.

Shakespeare's abundant interest in music is expressed in the talk of his characters about it, in the
number of songs which we are told that they sing —
the number actually sung was probably much larger,
because many must be unrecorded — in the much larger
number which they name without singing, and in many
other ways. He knew the songs of the people well —
their catches, rounds, jigs, and ballads, and he calls up
one after another of those most familiar in his day,—
*There Dwelt a Man in Babylon, Three Merry Men We
Be, Peg-a-Ramsey, Greensleeves,* etc. It would be
idle to claim that he was himself a skilled musician be-

[4] A very valuable discussion of this general subject is to be
found in E. W. Naylor's *Elizabethan Virginal Book,* from which
these conclusions are cited.

cause he used musical terms with intelligence, drew illustrations at pleasure from music, and showed himself saturated with the popular songs of his time.
Such a claim might involve us in the necessity for be-
lieving him skilled in many other arts and professions.
He must, however, have been fully in sympathy with
the musical mood of the time and have derived a genuine pleasure from it.

X

DANCING

The spirit of wholesome jollity in the country dances of Shakespeare's time makes them the most delightful of all the many which abounded then, although some of the more formal sort have much stately charm of their own. A quaint book of the period is dedicated to " Old Hall, taborer of Hertfordshire, and to his most invincible, weather-beaten, nut-brown tabor, which hath made bachelors and lasses dance round about the Maypole three score summers, one after another in order, and is not yet worm eaten." It gives an account of twelve Morris dancers in Hertfordshire, whose ages, added together, make twelve hundred years, and is meant chiefly to praise the Morris dancers of Hertfordshire, but gives pleasing glimpses of the part which dancing played in the life of the country people in other places:

" The court of kings is for stately measures; the city for light heels and nimble footing; western men for gambols, Lancashire for Hornpipes: Worcestershire for bagpipes: but Hertfordshire for a Morris-dance, puts down not only all Kent, but very near (if one had line enough to measure it) three quarters of Christendom. Never had Saint Sepulchre's a truer rain of bells; never did any silk weaver keep braver time; never could Beverley Fair give money

to a more sound taborer; nor ever had Robin Hood a more
deft Maid Marian."

To the Puritan, growing more and more intense
each day over the prevailing enjoyment of life, dancing was a cause of much depression. Stubbes, the
preacher, tells how it was used on the Sabbath from
morning until night in public assemblies and " fre-
quencies of people, men and women together with
pyping, fluting, dromming and such like in inticements
to wantonnesse and sin, together with their leapinges,
skippings & other unchast gestures, not a few: Being
used or rather abused in this sort, I utterly discom-
mend it." He adds generously, however: " But
upon the other side, being used in a man's private
chamber, or howse for his Godly solace and recreation
in the feare of God; or otherwise abroade with respect had to time, place and persons, it is in no respect to be disallowed."

Morris Dancing.

The Morris dance was widespread throughout England, and although especially associated in Elizabeth's
time with Mayday, was appropriate for any outdoor
season. It belonged naturally to the country, but was
popular at court, played its part in the entertainment
of the Queen on her progresses, and was used by London citizens in various festivities. The number taking part in it was apt to include at least six dancers,
all in gay attire, but the leader was most bravely
dressed and one of the dancers was often dressed as a

90, 91. MORRIS DANCERS.

173

girl. They frequently sang or whistled as they danced, the musical accompaniment of the bells and that of the piper making, together with the song and the dance, a combination of entertainment dear to the country sort.

Maypole Dances.

Stubbes, in a passage to be cited later, compares the "leaping and dancing" around the Maypole in Elizabethan villages to a heathen rite, seeming to imply a somewhat wild lack of order in the movements. It is probable that much of the dancing was of the haphazard sort, either by people dancing alone, somewhat in the fashion of a modern jig, or by couples — each couple using whatever dance was desired — or by dancing in circles. Undoubtedly a certain amount of spontaneity came out in the festivity, and made it all the more an expression of real life, as people of all ages, most of them untaught and crude, took part in the occasion.[1] One of the favourite musical accompaniments for the maypole dance was known as *Sellinger's Round* or the *Beginning of the World,* although the same music and dance were also much used at Christmas time. The music carried its own words and the combination was thus again as the countrymen loved it, that of song, instrumental music and the dance. Other dances popular in the country and among the lower classes elsewhere, were the jig, the brawl, the

[1] The picture facing p. III is probably of the time of Charles I, but will serve safely to illustrate the spontaneous informality of Mayday celebrations about the pole.

canary, the cushion dance, the trenchmore, the dump,
Tom Tiler, the hay, etc. Many of these dances were
used by the upper classes as well, and some even at
court, but there chiefly by way of relaxation from the
statelier sort. The jig was a frequent interlude between parts of a dramatic performance and usually
involved a song and some simple instrumental music
as well as a dance. There were often dialogue features also and suggestions of slight dramatic structure
in the jig itself. It constituted within itself a sufficiently varied entertainment and the jigs of Tarleton
and Kemp were widely famous. Music for one of the
Elizabethan jigs is found elsewhere,[2] and the steps
may be left, as they are in modern jigs, largely to the
ingenuity of the dancer, who realises the physical nimbleness and exuberance associated with the type. The
cushion dance took its name from the fact that the lady
put a cushion before the gentleman with whom she was
willing to dance. It was used both at court and outside. The dump was a very genteel but dolorous dance
associated with a song in which the lover lamented his
hard fate; the canary was one of the gayer dances.

Shakespeare furnishes an interesting allusion to the
vigorous country dances when he introduces into *The
Winter's Tale* three carters, three shepherds, three
neatherds, and three swineherds who call themselves
saltiers [leapers] and who wish to dance at a sheep-
shearing festival. Their dance is described by others
as " a gallimanfrey of gambols but they themselves

[2] p. 273.

declare that "if it is not too rough for some that know little but bowling, it will please plentifully." The shepherd in charge of the festival refuses them admission, but the messengers explains: "one three of them by their own report, sir, hath danced before the King, and not the worst of the three but jumps twelve foot and a half by the squier"; and the dancers are admitted.

Court Dancing.

A historian writing soon after Elizabeth's time has left this account of the dances which prevailed at her court:

"At a solemn dancing first you had the Grave measures, then the Corantoes and the Galliards, and this kept up with ceremony; and at length to Trenchmore and the Cushion dance. Then all the company danced, lord and groom, lady and kitchen maid, no distinction. So in our court in Queen Elizabeth's time, things went pretty well."

One cannot avoid scepticism, however, in regard to so democratic an ending of any court dancing, because contemporary records do little to suggest such taste on the Queen's part. The record of the dances used is, however, probably correct.

The measure was one of the more formal dances and belonged to the tradition of the English court. The pavan, thought to have been of Spanish origin, was perhaps the most picturesque of all court dances. It was not restricted to the court, but, even there, it belonged to the most ceremonious occasions. The more dignified instruments, such as the sackbut and hautboy, accompanied it; the most splendid robes were to be worn by those taking part, and the ladies of the court often wore, in dancing it, long trains which had to be held up by others. A famous treatise on dancing in that period declared that noblemen must dance the pavan gravely with cap and sword in hand; lawyers must wear their gowns, merchants must assume a gravity of demeanour, a " gravite posee "; and young girls must dance it with lowered eyes. It suggests the more stately movements of the minuet.

The galliard, the coranto, and the lavolta, all popular both at court and in the city, are described in some detail in the *Appendix* [3] and will be passed over more briefly here. The alman was also a very popular dance at court and elsewhere, and admitted of more than twenty varieties. The galliard was perhaps, the gayest of all, and being ready to dance a galliard seems to have been a half proverbial expression for all possible exuberance of mood. The galliard was called also the cinquepace, because of the five steps besides the caper into the air; the lavolta was swift, with more frequent capers; and the coranto was marked by a swift movement like running. Burton in his *Anatomy of Melancholy* alludes to " young men and maids flourishing in their age, fair and lovely to behold, well attired and of comely carriage, dancing

[3] pp. 263–274.

a Greek Galliard, and, as their dance requireth, keep their time, now running, now tracing, now apart, now altogether, now a curtesie, then a caper, etc.," and adds the words, " It is a pleasant sight."

XI

OUTDOOR AMUSEMENTS [1]

SIR PHILIP SIDNEY probably did more than any other Elizabethan to set the standard of physical grace and dexterity as a necessary part of the education of a gentleman, and he himself was much influenced by Italian ideals of courtly culture. Early in the sixteenth century Count Baldasarre Castiglione, the chief ornament of the court of Urbino and the model courtier for all cultured Europe, had written a book in which he set down all the virtues and accomplishments which he thought the ideal courtier ought to possess. The book became almost a Bible of courtly training and was quickly translated into many languages. It did not appear in English until after Sidney's death, but he doubtless knew it in the original and drew many of his precepts from it. In it Castiglione urges very earnestly upon the courtier the serious development of all knightly arts, and the book had tremendous influence upon Elizabeth's court in this matter as well as in others.

[1] Much of the dancing, and indeed much of the dramatic entertainment could be included under this title, but having been already treated, will not be discussed here except incidentally.

Some of Castiglione's injunctions came easily enough to the Elizabethan courtier, to whom the tilt and the tourney had long been familiar, and to whom the sword and dagger were parts of the everyday dress. The Queen, too, encouraged every form of knightly diversion. On each anniversary of her coronation her champion rode into the court lists and announced that he would uphold against all comers her title and right to England, France, Ireland, and Virginia; and many court ceremonials took on a similar suggestion of combat. There was much tilting, and fighting at the barriers, or tourneying, was bound up with court pageants of various kinds. The Queen, to be sure, seemed almost as much delighted to see acrobatic performances by professional athletes as the more graceful manœuvres of her courtiers. Laneham, who wrote a letter describing the Kenilworth festivities for the Queen in 1575, tells how a wonderful Italian acrobat amused her by giving an exhibition in " goings, turnings, tumblings, castings, hops, jumps, leaps, skips, springs, gambauds, somersaults, caprettings and flights forward, backward, sideways, downward, upward, and with sundry roundings, springs and circumflections," and adds: " As for the fellow, I cannot tell what to make of him, save that I may guess his back to be metalled like a lamprey that has no bones, but a line like a lute spring." Court records abound in items for similar amusements. The tilt and the tournament were, however, more characteristic of the court than those, because limited by law to people of rank, no one below the esquire being allowed to have part in them.

The Tournament.

The tournament, or tourney, was of course a relic of an earlier age, but was practised with much ceremony and elegance in Elizabeth's time. It was distinguished from the joust by being a conflict of many pairs of knights, whereas the joust was a single combat. When a tournament was in preparation, two barons, one the challenger and the other the defendant, set up each a pavilion with his arms before it, and to one or the other of these came all knights who were desirous of fighting on either side. Each of these knights also set up his arms, banner, and helmet at an appointed station outside the pavilion, and when these had been approved by the lord of the parade and the speakers, [these last being two or more in number] they were returned to the knights for use in the contest. This being done, the baron challenger moved forward to the parade or place for displaying the trappings of the tournament, planting his banner there and nailing his coat-of-arms upon it. Then followed the baron defendant and each of the lesser knights in turn, each retiring from the place when this task was completed, and waiting for the signal for further action. Next the king-at-arms, who, under the lord of the tournament, acted as master of ceremonies and as the chief standard-bearer, went with the heralds from one pavilion to the other crying aloud, " To achievement, es-

quires, to achievement! Come forth, knights and esquires. Come forth!" At this summons the two
chief barons, challenger and defendant, attended by
their pages, came forward to the lists within the parade, and faced each other: then each of the followers
on either side, facing one another in pairs, and each
attended, like the barons, by his page. Each knight
was provided with a pointless sword, and a short heavy
staff known as a truncheon was fastened to his side.
The contest took place at a point where certain parti-
tions called barriers had been set up to keep the op-
posing knights from pressing one upon the other too
dangerously; hence the term " fighting at the barriers,"
which is used so often in court records to describe the
tournaments taking place before Elizabeth.[2] Ladies
often bestowed the prizes for the contest, and the king-
at-arms and heralds claimed the helmets of all the
knights taking part.

Tilting.

Tilting differed from the tournament in being a contest not of one knight with another, but of each knight
for the greatest success in thrusting his lance through
a ring which was suspended at a point which he must
pass. Each was on horseback and was provided with
a long lance. The ring was operated by a spring and
the thrusting of the lance through it released it from
its fastening, so that it became the possession of the
knight. The victor was the one who at the end of

[2] In the picture facing p. 190 the barriers do not appear.

92. HOODMAN'S BLIND.

(From Strutt's "Sports and Pastimes.")

93. TILTING AT THE RING, ETC.
(From Strutt's "Sports and Pastimes.")

94. FENCING IN A DUEL.

the contest had the largest number of rings. Success required not only a sure aim but a very swift and vigorous assault upon the ring, and the colloquialism in use to-day by which we speak of " going full tilt " into some enterprise or adventure is doubtless a survival from the phraseology for this form of amusement. Tilting was slightly less ceremonious than the tourney in Elizabeth's day, and lacked the more intense interest of a man-to-man contest, but it was brilliant as a spectacle, with the gay trappings of men and horses, and was full of excitement.

Fencing.

Fencing, although also in favour with the nobility, was a more widespread form of amusement outside the court than tilting or the tourney, because not restricted to the upper classes. That such exercise, with the sword and dagger, as well as with foils, was held to be a serious art, besides being an amusement, is shown in this extract from a letter of advice written by Sir Philip Sidney to his brother.

" When you play at weapons, I would have you get thick caps and bracers [gloves] and play your play lustily; for, indeed, tricks and dalliance are nothing in earnest: for the time of the one and of the other greatly differ. And use as well the blow as the thrust. It is good in itself and, besides, increaseth your breadth and strength and will make you a strong man at the tourney and barriers. First in any case, practice with the single sword, and then with the dagger. Let no day pass without an hour or two of such exercise."

Morning seems to have been the favourite time for fencing, and among the middle classes there were many contests in tavern yards, and elsewhere. The practice comes out in many plays of the time,— both in the allusions made to it and in the illustrations of it included in the action of the play.

Archery.

Archery was one of the most graceful of Elizabethan pastimes and had the advantage of being suitable for both sexes. Elizabeth herself was highly accomplished with the bow and arrow, and is reported to have killed three or four deer with a crossbow in a single morning when on a visit to Cowdray, a country seat belonging to one of her nobility. Formal archery, contests, where a target was set up for a group of archers, was a favourite form of amusement for the middle classes; and Strutt, who is the chief authority for Elizabethan sports, has furnished some account of the conditions under which it was then played. He explains that each archer wore a bracer or close sleeve too short to crease, so that the arm might be strengthened; and that a shooting glove protected the fingers. The bow was made from wood carefully chosen for its seasoning, and so shaped as to taper from the middle towards each end, the yew wood being reckoned the best for it. The bow-string could be made of hemp, flax, or silk, and the arrow consisted of a *stele* or wand. with feathers at the head.

Oak and ash were considered good material for the

95. THE QUINTAIN AND A WATER JOUST.

(From Strutt's "Sports and Pastimes.")

96. TRAINED ANIMALS.

(From Strutt's "Sports and Pastimes.")

wand, and goose feathers the best for the head of the
arrow.

Hunting.

The term hunting can be used comprehensively of
many Elizabethan sports, whether the game was pur-

97. HUNTING.

sued by one means or another, as by the falcon, with
bow and arrow, with the musket, etc. The extent to
which it was practised and the art which was associated
with dexterity in the practice, is suggested by the title
of the treatise on hunting which George Turberville
published in 1575, about the middle of Elizabeth's

reign. The title, even as given here, is abridged:

" The noble Arte of Veneries or Hunting. Wherein is handled and set out the Vertues, Nature and Properties of five sundrie Chaces together with the order and maner how to Hunte and kill every one of them. Translated and collected for the pleasure of all Noblemen and Gentlemen our of the best . . . authors which have written any thing concerning the same . . . with such order and proper termes as are used here in this noble Realme of England."

The book contained fifty-three illustrations for the clearer instruction of those ambitious to excel. A surviving copy is bound in stag skin, figured with stags, and has silver corners, its elegance showing the high esteem in which it was held. The picture given on the title page is presented here.

Hawking.

In the same year in which this volume appeared, the energetic Turberville brought out another on the popular form of hunting known as hawking or falconry. It bore the title:

The Booke of Faulconrie or Hauking, FOR THE ONELY DElight and pleasure of all Noblemen and Gentlemen:
Collected out of the best aucthors, afvvell Italians as Frenchmen, and some Englifh practifes withall concernyng Faulconrie,

98. REDUCED FACSIMILE OF TITLE.

Hawking or falconry was one of the oldest of English pastimes, and it is said that when Edward the

Third invaded France he took thirty falconers with him to care for his hawks. The sport derives its two names from the fact that the hawk or falcon, being itself a bird of prey, was used by the hunter to assist him in pursuing other birds and game. The hawk was carried on the wrist of the hunter and was kept blinded with a hood or cap until he was needed for action; the expression *hoodwinked* is derived from this latter practice. Leather straps, which were fastened to the legs of the falcon, were attached at the other end to the hand of the hunter, and were known as *jesses*. When the hawk was in flight he was loosed on a long thread known as the *creance* and he was brought down by the drawing of this thread. He wore bells placed on leather rings, or *bewits,* about his legs, and the bells were selected with much care by a skilful falconer, to form a certain musical sequence of sound. They had to be light enough not to interfere with the mounting of the hawk and not too full in their sound.

Strutt in his *Sports and Pastimes* reminds us that freedom for the commons to indulge in hawking was one of the privileges wrested by them from King John in the Magna Charta, the right having been held until that time only by the nobility. Even in Shakespeare's time, however, there was much of the feeling of caste privilege in connection with hawking, and certain sorts were held appropriate for certain orders even among the nobility themselves, as for example the ger-falcon for the sovereign, the rock falcon for a duke, the goshawk for a yeoman, the sparrow hawk for a

priest, etc.; but it seems doubtful whether these distinctions were carefully observed. Quails, partridges,
rooks, and innumerable other birds were among the
objects of pursuit in falconry, and the hunter might be
either on horseback or on foot. Strutt records a tale
of how King Henry the Eighth was hawking on foot
in a wood, and, in leaning upon his hunting pole to
cross a filthy pool, broke the pole and fell into the
water, from which he was extricated with much incon-
venience.

Quintain.[3]

Quintain was much like tilting; indeed tilting at
the quintain was a favourite sport combining the two
forms of contest; and some have surmised that both
tilting and the tournament were developed from quintain, which is known to have been a very old game.
The name was derived from the target or object of
attack, which might be a board or the figure of a man,
as seen in the illustrations, or any one of various other
objects; and a weapon practically like the lance used in
tilting was employed in making the attack upon it.
Whatever it was, the target was so arranged as to turn
violently and strike its assailant if the thrust at it was
not made in precisely the proper fashion; and the
amusement over the penalties for failure at this were a
large element in the popularity of the game. It could
be played on foot, from a boat, or on horseback. The
illustrations here given show only the first two meth-

[3] See picture facing p. 184.

ods. Stowe, in his Elizabethan *Survey of London,* tells in these words of the game as he saw it played:

" I have seen a quintain set upon Cornhill by Leadenhall, where the attendants of the lords of the merry disports have run and made great pastime; for he that hit not the board end of the quintain was laughed to scorn and he that hit it full, if he rode not the faster, had a sound blow upon his neck with a bag full of sand hanged on the other end."

The Exhibition and Baiting of Animals.[4]

Another group of Elizabethan amusements, and one popular with all classes, involved the exhibition of animals, either to show the tricks which they had acquired or to bait them in some way too cruel to be tolerated to-day outside of Spain.

The training of animals for public performance reached a high state of development in Elizabeth's time. The famous " Banks, the Showman " had a horse which he had brought to such wonderful skill that both master and horse were held to be servants of the devil. Jugglers, the descendants of the old travelling entertainers of the Middle Ages, trained animals of various kinds, and the juggler with his " well-educated ape " performing tricks over a chain seems to have been familiar figures, not only at the country and city fairs, but on the stages of the theatres.

The baiting of bulls and bears with dogs was a custom which Elizabeth found when she ascended the throne, and she helped to keep it alive by her patronage,

[4] See picture facing p. 185.

using such entertainment both early in her reign and late, even for the diversion of foreign notables visiting at her court. The baiting of thirteen bears by bandogs will be remembered as one of the entertainments provided for her at Kenilworth, and Laneham's account of it, quoted elsewhere, shows that the spectacle was not lacking in gruesomeness according to modern tastes. Outside of courtly circles, however, the fashion of animal baiting was still more popular. Circular enclosed places, known as bear gardens and providing scaffolds for the spectators, were located in various suburban pleasure grounds, and, as already said, bear baiting became an alternate form of entertainment with the drama in more than one theatre, limiting the structure of the theatre to such conditions as could easily be used or changed when bear-baiting was in order. Paris Garden on the Bankside was the most famous of all the bear gardens. Paul Hentzner, the German traveller, whose diary has been several times quoted in other connections, has left this account of a bear baiting at which he was present:

"There is a place built in the form of a theatre which serves for baiting of bulls and bears. They are fastened behind and then worried by great English bulldogs; but not without risque to the dogs from the horns of one and the teeth of the other. . . . To this entertainment there often follows that of whipping a blinded bear, which is performed by five or six men standing circularly with whips, which they exercise upon him without any mercy, as he cannot escape, because of his chain; he defends himself with all his force and skill, throwing down all that come within his

99. TOURNAMENTS AND THE HERALDS (above).
(From Strutt's " Sports and Pastimes.")

100, 101. ROYAL HERALDS IN THEIR TABARDS.

(From illuminated documents of the period.)

102. DOGBERRY AND VERGES.

103. ANNE OF DENMARK.
Wife of James I.

reach and are not active enough to get out of, and tearing the whips out of their hands and breaking them."

Cock Fighting.

Cock fighting is obviously an old English custom associated especially with Shrove Tuesday, and it is said that even school children were set on by their teachers that day to persecute a hen or a cock brought into the schoolroom for the purpose. Later on the sport began to be practised on a larger scale. Certainly by the time of Henry VIII, a cockpit had been built for the entertainment of royalty at Whitehall Palace, and Strutt reports that James the First indulged himself in attendance upon cock fights twice every week. Strutt explains further that it was the fashion in the larger cockpits to set from fourteen to sixteen cocks to fighting one another in pairs, until about half of them are killed; then, to divide the survivors again into pairs, set them to fighting and so continue until only one survived. Cock fighting, like bear baiting, was often shown at theatres or in gardens which were used at other times for the drama.

Lotteries.

The fashion of drawing lots or taking chances at some very desirable object was carried to a highly extravagant length in Elizabeth's time; and then, as now at benevolent fairs, was fostered with the justification of good works to be done from the proceeds. Stowe in his *Survey of London* tells of a lottery conducted

in St. Paul's Churchyard, which began there at the
west door in January, 1569, and lasted without inter-
mission day or night until the sixth of May. It was
described in the notice advertising it as a " very rich
lottery, general without any Blankes, contayning a
great No. of good prices as well of redy money
as of Plate, etc." Another in Paul's Churchyard is
recorded in 1586 for a " marvellous rich and beautifull
armour," and a special building was constructed to
transact the business connected with that. That venture was concluded within two or three days, lasting
continuously, however, through the intervening nights.

Country Sports for the Masses.
Bowling.

Bowling was much played by villagers on a close-
cut turf; hence the expression, " bowling green." The
popularity of the game is suggested by the village laws
regulating the hours when it could be played. There
was some practice of it by the nobility in indoor alleys.
The curate in *Love's Labour's Lost* will be remembered as " a marvellous good neighbour and a very
good bowler " in spite of his failure in the rôle of
Alexander the Great; also the allusion in *The Winter's
Tale* to the country people who " know little but bowling."

Hoodman Blind.[5]

Hoodman blind seems rather a game for children
than for adults but was popular as a Christmas " gam-
[5] See picture facing p. 182.

bol " or game for all.   It suggests the modern blind-
man's buff, as one person was blinded and forced to capture another to take his place, before he can be released. The name was derived from the hood worn
backwards by the one blinded, and the game was a
somewhat vigorous one, as the person wearing the
hood was knocked about from one spot to another by
those who could see.

Mayday Observances.

The most interesting of all the country sports were
those already mentioned briefly in the chapter on
dancing, as being connected with Mayday. They oc-
curred not always on the first day of May, but usually
on some day in the earlier part of the month. They
were the outgrowth of a custom very old and seemingly
world-wide, of welcoming the spring with some special
festivity. The custom is still observed in many parts
of England; in some places, by more or less direct survival of the custom from early times; in others, through
the energy of interested folk-lore lovers. The Elizabethan way of observing it may be described in the
words of Stubbes:

" Against May, Whitsuntide or some other time of the
year, every parish, town and village, assemble themselves
together, both men, women and children, and either all
together, or dividing themselves into companies, they go,
some to the woods and groves, some to the hills and moun-
tains, some to one place, some to another, and in the morning they return bringing with them birch boughs and

branches of trees, to deck their assembly withal. . . . But
their chiefest jewel they bring from thence is their twenty
or forty yoke of oxen, every ox having a sweet nosegay of
flowers tied to the tip of his horns, and these oxen draw
home this May-pole, which is covered all over with flowers
and herbs, bound round about with strings, from the top to
the bottom, and sometime pointed with variable colours,
with two or three hundred men, women, and children following it with great devotion. And thus being reared up,
with handkerchiefs and flags streaming on the top, they
strew the ground about, bind green boughs about it, set
up summer halls, bowers, and arbours hard by it; and then
fall they to banquet and feast, to leap and dance about it
as the heathen did at the dedication of their idols."

The dance about the maypole here mentioned by
Stubbes was the most characteristic feature of the
Mayday, though often more æsthetically carried out
than as here described. The form of the Maypole dance which we follow most often to-day, however, involves a continuous circling about the pole,
the circle being made up chiefly of girls and boys in
alternation. Each holds in his hand, the end of a
long ribbon from the top of the pole, and weaves it in
close to the pole, along with those of his companions,
as he keeps constantly moving around, the circle being
gradually contracted as the ribbon is woven about
the pole. At the end the many-coloured ribbons are
all woven in and the pole is completely covered. The
Lord and Lady of the May were part of the celebration, pre-eminence being especially given to the Lady
or Queen. The Robin Hood group — Robin Hood

himself, Maid Marian his sweetheart, Little John,
Friar Tuck, etc.— were frequently associated with the
Mayday festivities, Robin and Marian being often
the Lord and Lady of the May.   The enthusiasm for
Robin Hood was of course a strong tradition with the

104.   A FISHERMAN WITH HIS ANGLE.
(Temp. James I)

English countryman, and when Robin and his band
were identified with the annual spring festival everything conspired to make the occasion delightful.
Bishop Latimer, in the reign of Edward the Sixth,
describing his visit to a certain place on the day set for
Mayday observance, tells how he came to church to

preach, found the door locked, and, after much searching for the key, came upon some one who explained with impatient emphasis: —" Syr, this is a busy day with us, we cannot hear you; it is Robin Hoode's day; the parish are gone abroad to gather for Robin Hoode: I pray you let them." The bishop adds in conclusion: " I was fayne, therefore, to give place to Robin Hood." [6]

[6] The Morris dances, also closely associated with the celebration of Mayday, are discussed in the chapter on Dancing p. 171.

105. THE JOVIAL TINKER.

There was a jovial tinker,
Who was a good ale drinker.
He never was a shrinker,
Believe me this is true.
And he came from the wold of Kent
When all his money was gone and spent
Which made him look like Jack-a-lent.
And Joan's ale is new,
And Joan's ale is new my boys,
And Joan's ale is new.

Miscellaneous.

A great variety of other outdoor games might be cited, more than one of them having the same name by which it is known to-day — as leapfrog, tennis, etc. Still other varieties of popular diversions were these suggestive of vaudeville, circuses, and entertainment at county fairs to-day.

Perhaps the description of " The Tinker of Trotman " in *The Two Maides of Moreclacke* is as typical of his inclusive sort as any, and may serve to end the account of this motley of entertainment.

" This, Madame, is the tinker of Trotnam. I have seene him licke out burning fire-brands with his tongue, drink twopence from the bottom of a full bottle of ale, fight with a masty [a mastiff] and stroke his mustachoes with his bloody-bitten fist, and sing as merrily as the soberest cherester [chorister]."

XII

ELIZABETHAN DRESS [1]

In dress, as in all other things, Queen Elizabeth set the fashions, and her own extravagance there knew no bounds. She is said to have had nearly two thousand dresses, chosen from the costumes of many countries, and Lord Melville, visiting at court, reported her own statement that she had the clothes of every nationality. He adds that each day while he was there she wore the clothes of a different nation, one day the English; another, the French; another, the Italian, etc. After a time she asked of him which costume became her best, and when he replied the Italian, she was well pleased, because the Italian net and bonnet showed the reddish yellow hair of which she was proud. She was fond, too, of decking her hair with jewels, wore a jewelled stomacher, many rings and necklaces, and ornamented her gowns with all possible elaboration. Hentzner has left a description of a costume worn by her on one occasion when he saw her giving a royal audience,

[1] Account is also taken of the early Jacobean fashions, but the Elizabethan covered a much larger proportion of Shakespeare's life and changes from it after James's accession were not very radical. See also *Costume Index* in Part II.

" That day she was dressed in white silk bordered with pearls of the size of beans, and over it a mantle of black silk, with silver threads; her Train was very long and the end of it borne by a Marchioness: instead of a chain she had an oblong collar of gold and jewels . . . her right hand sparkling with rings and jewels. . . ."

There is every indication that the nobility and the middle classes, and even those below, pushed their extravagance in dress astonishingly near to the Queen's. Stubbes the Puritan, wrote unintentionally in his *Anatomie of Abuses* the most authoritative book on Elizabethan dress, while setting out some of the abuses of the fashions of the day. He declares that while vanity in dress is a common fault among nations, " there is not any people under the Zodiacke of heaven, how clownish, rural, or brutish soever, that is so poisoned with this arsnecke of pride" as the English are. The prevailing neglect of considerations of caste in dress weighed heavily upon him and he asserted that the lower orders even surpassed the nobility in the splendour of their attire, " russling in Silks, Velvets, Satens, Damasks, Taffeties, Gold, Silver, and what not, with their swords, daggers, and rapiers guilte and reguilte, burnished and costly ingrauen, with all things else that any noble, honourable, or worshipfull man doth, or may weare, so as the one cannot easily be discerned from the other." Elsewhere he repeats the charge and adds, " This I count a great confusion and generall disorder: God be merciful unto us."

Another characteristic of Elizabethan ways of dress has already been touched upon in what was said of the Queen's costumes — the ambition to follow as many foreign fashions as possible. Lyly, in a prologue already quoted, calls attention to the variety of countries which must supply the fashions of a gallant's dress. In Greene's dialogue called *A quip for an upstart Courtier, or a quaint dispute between velvet breeches and cloth breeches;* Velvet breeches, the Englishman who follows the Italian fashions, is addressed by his barber in this fashion: —

" Sir, will you have your worship's haire cut after the Italian maner, shorte and round, and then frounst [crimped] with the curling yrons to make it look like a halfe moone in a miste? Or will you be Frenchified with a love locke downe to your shoulders, wherein you may weare your mistresse favour. The English cut is base, and gentlemen scorne it, novelty is daintye: speak the word sir, and my sissars are ready to execute your worship's wil."

King James, years later, in his *Counterblaste of Tobacco,* scores the English for the same tendency:

" Do we not dayly see that a man can no sooner bring over from beyond the seas any new forme of apparell, but that hee can not bee thought a man of spirit that would not presently [at once] imitate the same . . . like apes counterfeiting the manners of others to our owne destruction."

The Elizabethan ruff, worn well into the Jacobean period by both sexes, was apparently the main object of pride for the wearer and of attack by those assailing the vanities of dress. Stubbes, in railing at them, tells of the houses for trimming them, the starching houses, the heated putting-stick to give them their final shape, etc. They were made on frames which were often very elaborate structures. Stubbes calls the starch which went into them " the Devil's liquor," and the ruffs themselves " cartwheels in the Devil's chariot of pride."

Much that was said about the Revels' costumes for dramatic performances at court applies to Elizabethan dress in general, although on a scale which is naturally reduced. The Elizabethan eye was lavish in its indulgence in colour, and the richest materials seem to have been taken for granted. Both sexes used silks, velvets, furs, laces, embroideries, feathers, etc., in profusion.

Men of the upper classes wore, for the most part, the doublet and hose, and full semi-circular capes or long cloaks when abroad. They used the richest materials — silks, velvets, etc.— trimmed their doublets almost as extravagantly as women did their bodices, stiffened their doublets with crinoline and stays, and altogether sacrificed almost as much comfort to fashions as Elizabethan women did.

Stubbes declares, what seems likely enough from the portraits, that many doublets were too tight and stiff with stays to admit of their wearers' stooping; and Florio's testimony here cited seems borne out by the portraits of Southampton, and others:

" To become slender in waist and to have a straight spagnolized body, what pinching, what griding, what cingling will they not endure; yea sometimes with yron plates with whalebones and other such trash that their very skin and quick flesh is eaten into and consumed to the bones."

The variety of jewels which they wore was less than with women, but they were given to large and heavy gold chains, to jewels in their hats, rings, etc.

Men's vanity as to personal appearance is brought out in allusions to their custom of carrying mirrors. The tobacco box and dial were also among the many articles taken about as a part of the equipment for social life and enjoyment. This description of a gallant's equipment is in point:

> " That never walkes without his looking glasse
> In a tobacco box or diall set,
> That he may privately conferre with it."

The elaborate cloaks or robes worn by court officials in state processions are shown in several of the pictures. A sword and dagger, or a sword and a rapier, were put on as a part of the dress. Where stockings were worn, as with the Venetian hose,[2] they were of silk, and often in bright colours. Shoes were usually low, and of russet, velvet, leather, etc. Pumps were much in fashion; so were low shoes which were higher in front; and buckles, rosettes, etc., were the trimming for men's shoes as well as for women's, heels were high and of cork for the most fashionable. The hair was worn cut close at the top of the head and

2 See p. 282.

left full about the ears. Common-place books, in which a pleasing sonnet, an epigram or other desirable gleanings from the talk of the day might be written down, were also a proper accessory for a gentleman. Much of the briefer poetry of the time circulated only in this fashion.

The accessories of a thoroughly well-kept woman's toilet seem almost beyond number. A university play of the period does, however, make this jocular attempt:

"Five hours ago I set a dozen maids to attire a boy like a nice gentlewoman; but there is such doing with their looking glasses, pinning, unpinning, unsetting, formings and conformings, painting blue veins and cheeks; such stir with sticks and combs, carcanets,[1] dressings, kurls, frills, squares, busts,[2] bodies, scarfs, necklaces, rebatoes,[3] borders, tires,[4] fans, palisadoes,[5] puffs, ruffs, cuffs, muffs, pulses,[6] . . . partlets,[7] frislets,[8] bandlets, fillets, crosslets,[9] . . . armlets, bracelets, and so many lets, that yet she's scarce dressed to the girdle: and now there is such calling for fardingales,[10] kirtles,[11] . . . shoe ties, etc., that seven pedlars' shops — nay, all Stonebridge fair will scarce furnish her. A ship is sooner rigged by far than a gentlewoman made ready."

[1] Ornamental collars or necklaces or supports for ruffs.
[2] Corsets or stays, especially the stiff strip down the front.
[3] Stiff collars or underpropping for ruffs.
[4] Attire.
[5] Part of a head dress.
[6] Apparently trifles of the toilet, the word being used jocularly.
[7] Neckwear sometimes reaching to the chest.
[8] Small ruffles.
[9] Small crosses used as ornaments.
[10] Stage skirts set out with hoops.
[11] Smaller skirts.

But even this enumeration may be supplemented. Marston has an allusion in one of his plays to Dr. Plasterface, who is " the most exquisite," not only " in forging of veins," but in the " sprightening of eyes, blanching and bleaching of teeth that ever made an old lady gracious by torch light." Whether the Elizabethan women were actually more alert in their search for beauty than women are to-day, or were only more fully described, may be an open question, but the picture of one of them in farthingale and ruff, and the description just cited of the intricacies of her toilet goes far to justify the gloomy strictures of Stubbes:

"When they have all these goodly robes upon them, women seeme to be the smallest part of themselves, not naturall women but artificial women: not women of flesh & blod but rather puppets or mawmets of rags and clowts [clouts] compact together."

PART II

*A Guide for Shakespeare Productions
and Pageants*

I

THE PAGEANT — INTRODUCTION

THE ideal for every pageant is that it shall represent
a community, not merely an institution or a single organisation. Whether themselves representing a school,
a college, a club, or some other group, its designers
should draw the neighbourhood into it, and as far as
possible, make the occasion the expression of neighbourhood interest and pleasure. The community is
the natural unit for a pageant; both because numbers
widen the possible range of colour and action, and because they heighten the festival spirit. In every community, too, the artistic, literary, educational, com-
mercial and other interests should, as far as possible,
join together to make the pageant a success, so that
it shall represent both the support and the participation
of the city, or town or country neighbourhood as a
whole. The difficulty in bringing about such participation is much smaller than the traditional social barriers
and the pressure of the day's work for most people
might make us believe. The instinct for pleasure
and festival lurks somewhere in most of us and will
usually respond to a tactful appeal. The difficulties
in the way of expense, costuming, and lack of time

for memorising and rehearsing parts may be reduced to negligible proportions by wise committees, and the poorest and busiest participants may be given non-speaking parts for which very simple costumes are required. A large proportion of the characters in the procession would naturally have no lines at all, and many would represent social types, orders of workingmen, etc., rather than definite Elizabethan individuals. Many could take part in the games or dances, all easily learned by those whose tastes tend that way. Trainers for both should be provided by the central committee. Even with these, however, it is of the greatest importance that each should have a human understanding of the part he is assuming, and be able to keep within its lines in his movements and also in the general character of his talk, if he is later to mingle in costume among the spectators. Teachers who are helping in the preparations for the pageant, or others acquainted with Shakespeare and his times, could do nothing more helpful than to meet each a group of such prospective participants for one evening or more, to tell the story of the play in which those present are involved, and read parts of certain striking scenes; or, where certain historical personages are to be represented, to explain the historical background, interpret the characters, etc.

It is suggested that the spirit of the occasion will be greatly helped by providing, near the gates of admission, very simple costumes which could be rented by spectators for a small cost, and worn over other garments. Some one-piece garments easily adjusted would be best for this and some effective headgear might be devised to go with it if desired.

Uniformity in Shakespeare festivals is of course highly undesirable and the possibilities for variation are almost unlimited. What follows is meant to be merely suggestive of some of these possibilities. Knowing Shakespeare and his plays better is the natural motive behind such a festival, and the advantage of suggesting the environment in which he and his work developed is too obvious to need argument. No man was ever more fully a part of his age. For this reason the suggestions here include not only the performance of plays or parts of plays by him, but the presentation of as many of the people and activities of his England as possible. Sir Thomas Lucy, the Queen and her courtiers, the Lord Mayor of London and his guilds, Shakespeare's fellow actors and dramatists, even the beggars, ballad singers, bear-wards, dancers, musicians, etc., show us the life of which he was a part and which he so strongly reflected in his plays.

The Procession.

This may begin with the coronation procession of Queen Elizabeth in 1558 and move forward gradually with its suggestions of court life and London until it shifts to Stratford for the birth of Shakespeare in 1564. The events, proved and traditional, in Shakespeare's life, up to his leaving Stratford about 1586, may be presented then with as much social background as possible. From this point the scene could properly be transferred to London and continue there until Shakespeare's retirement to Stratford. This more realistic part of the procession as here outlined would close with his death. His relation to the life represented should be repeatedly emphasised by having him appear at an appropriate age in each of the more important groups with which he was associated in his time, and more than once with single individuals, as with Southampton, or Burbage, or others. Another section of the procession could fitly represent the characters of Shakespeare's plays, the groups from the several plays appearing in the order in which the plays were written, so far as this order is known or reasonably conjectured.[1]

Activities.

The Elizabethan activities, involving chiefly recreations of different sorts, may be shown before or after the procession, or without it, although the characters needed to participate in them would go far towards making a successful procession, being effective figures for variety and movement. The activities include such diversions as may be used for a Stratford fair or for London pleasure grounds. Account must be taken at the beginning, of the size of the grounds, of the approximate number of spectators for whom preparations are to be made, and of the types of activities adapted

[1] See p. 115 for chronological table of Shakespeare's plays.

to these conditions. Dances require ample space but may be watched either at close range or at a distance. Ballad singers may mingle in a crowd of moderate size and sing and sell their ballads there, but the tavern scenes from *Henry IV* in a tavern-like booth could be given only for a small group placed near enough for the words to be heard.

In a general way the scale of suggestion is large enough to be used in a city pageant commanding ample grounds, vast audiences, and a considerable sum of money for preparations — possibilities not to be ignored when one of our American cities has, twice in the past eight years, spent ninety thousand dollars on a pageant; and St. Louis has ventured still further in its scale of elaboration. Enormous sums are also being provided elsewhere for pageants now in preparation. On the other hand, it is to be expected that most celebrations will be on a far simpler scale than these, and the suggestions provided here have fully as much reference to the more modest undertakings as to the elaborate ones.

It is of great importance that the pageant should make one definite impression, and not develop in a straggling fashion by the chance addition of one feature and then of another. Every varied element of life and action employed should converge directly to emphasis upon Shakespeare himself. It is necessary to consider too from the beginning, the proportions of the two sexes to be involved. In a pageant which is for the public and is to be presented entirely by women,

or women and girls, very careful choice should be made
of characters and activities offering the fewest difficulties in costuming, and much can be accomplished towards success in this way. Ideally, of course, both
sexes should be included in any pageant attempting
the presentation of Elizabethan life in varied aspects;
and, except here and there in boarding schools for
girls, it ought to be possible to include both, at least
by joining groups which have been separately trained.
If, however, the pageant needs to be carried out chiefly
by girls, it is possible to compose the procession chiefly
of such Elizabethan dignitaries as would naturally
wear robes or gowns on occasions of state, to include
in it large numbers of the ladies of the courts of Elizabeth and of James I, and to emphasise the activities
which are chiefly adapted to girls. Officials of the
crown, of the church, and of the universities would
naturally be wearing robes of state in a formal procession; so would the Lord Mayor and aldermen of
London, the mayor and aldermen of Stratford, the
countless representatives of London guilds, the doctors, the lawyers, etc. Even at the worst, a few
proper wearers of the doublet and hose could be found
to give this Elizabethan touch to the costuming on
a public occasion; Maypole dances, milkmaids, country and city women of various social types and orders could be very interestingly reproduced, and it
would be well worth while for a pageant, entirely restricted to using the one sex, to make some aspects of
woman's life, as presented in Shakespeare's plays and

shown in the Elizabethan age, furnish the organising idea for a procession and for most of the entertainment later. Such a limitation of activities is, however, by no means necessary.

Distinction is made in this volume between fact and tradition, and between authorised and imaginative portraits. It is important that these distinctions should be kept clear and definitely indicated in any explanatory booklet or program put into the hands of spectators. Such a program is of too great value to be omitted, and can easily be made a source of financial profit, even though sold for a very small sum.

Much of the material included in Part II of this book is drawn directly from Elizabethan and Jacobean documents, and is presented with only occasional modernisation of spelling. It ought to be useful in giving a breath of the times, in showing the Elizabethan sense of spectacle, and in providing the names of actual participants in actual festivities of those times. There is no thought that all the state processions of Elizabeth's time, which are recorded here, will be reproduced. Possibly none of them could be given in full detail: in various features too they overlap. Each probably contains terms unfamiliar to the general reader, but as much glossarial aid as space permits is given and for the rest the reader is referred to a large dictionary.

Wherever there is any danger that spectators shall not understand a character or a group, some symbol or even a title should be carried. This applies especially to the workingmen's guilds, but is applicable in all connections.

It has not been possible to find authentic portraits for all the persons appropriate to appear in such a procession; and the limits of the book do not permit the inclusion of all those found. It has seemed best, however, to name as many as possible of the persons involved in such a setting, and to leave to the discretion of the pageant-maker the decision as to whether to go beyond those for whom authentic portraits can be found.

II

THE PROCESSION

A

Elizabeth's Triumphal Procession Through London on the Way to Her Coronation.[1]

[Condensed from state records.]

Heralds, page 191

Serving men	Knights
Queen's Pensioners	Lords
Gentlemen, page 299	Aldermen

Sergeants-at-Arms

Heralds in coat-armour, page 191

Lord Mayor with scepter, page 226

Lord Chamberlain with the royal sword, page 226

Queen borne in litter by richly dressed footmen

Lord's men and knights in livery, page 37

Earl of Suffolk	Baron of Hunsdon, p. 222
Earl of Ormond	Lord Wentworth
Sir John Perrott	Lord Darcy
William Lord Howard	Lord Cliche

[1] References given to pages refer either to illustrations and descriptive matter on those pages or to illustrations facing them.

215

Lord Buckhurst, page 222

Sir Edward Dimmock, Knight, Queen's Champion by office —" in faire complete armour," mounted upon a beautiful courser, richly trapped in cloth of gold and wearing splendid gauntlet.

William Paulitt, Marquis of Manchester and Lord Treasurer. The Earl of Arundel as Lord Steward, " with a silver wand a yard long, commanding everybody," page 226.

Sir Robert Southwell, Knight, Master of the Rolls.

Sir Edward Warner, Lieutenant of the Tower

Sir Thomas Carden, " deviser of banquets and banqueting houses and Master of the Revels."

Ambassadors   Archbishops and Bishops

Lords Spiritual   from outside London

Gentlemen Ushers   Bishops of London, etc.,

Dean of St. Paul's, page 301

Canons and Prebendaries

A thousand men in harness [armour], gunners, etc., with sheets of mail and corslets, morrice piles and ten great pieces carried through the city, with drums and trumpets sounding, and two morrice dancings and in a cart two white bears.

Commons [in Parliament robes]

Speaker, Knights, Citizens and Burgesses

Lord Mayor with scepter, page 226

26 Aldermen

Recorder of London   Town Clerk

Sheriff of London   Common Sergeant

Chamberlain of London   Attendants of the Mayor

Esquires
- Sword Bearers
- Common Hunt
- Common Crier
- Water Bailiff

Coroner of London
3 Sergeant Carvers
3 Sergeants of the Chamber
Sergeant of the Channel
Yeoman of the Channel
4 Yeomen of the Waterside

Under-Water Bailiff
2 Yeomen of the Chamber
3 Meal Weighers
2 Yeomen of the wood wharves
The Sword bearer's man
2 Common Huntsmen
Common Criersmen
2 Water Bailiff's men
The Carver's man

MUSICIANS OF THE QUEEN'S HOUSEHOLD

17 Trumpeters
6 Sackbut Players
3 Drummers
2 Players on the Flute
2 Lutanists
1 Rebeck Player
3 Viol Players

2 Harpers
2 Players on the Virginal
2 Makers of Instruments
8 Singers
6 Singing Children
9 Minstrels
7 " Musician strangers "

THE QUEEN'S SUITORS OR THEIR AMBASSADORS

The Prince of Sweden
The Duke of Holstein
Guzman de Alfarache as Ambassador of Philip II of Spain
The Earl of Arran [in Scotch costume]

Ambassadors of Eric, the King of Sweden
Philibert of Savoy
Charles IX of France
Duke d'Alençon
Charles, Archduke of Austria

Robert Devereux, Earl of   Robert Cecil
   Essex, page 223   Earl of Leicester, page 97
A few Puritan men, women and children in Puritan
   costume — the men with thoughtful and somewhat belligerent looks.

Shakespeare's Earlier Years in Stratford.

Facts.

[Facts are to be in some way carefully distinguished from
traditions. The facts should march solidly forward and the
traditions may run or limp on the side in somewhat inci-
dental fashion, or floats may be used for them, although one
method of presenting them should certainly be followed
throughout. In any case it will be best to have the title
Tradition borne by some figure connected with each one.]

The parish register of the Stratford church carried
   open at the page where the date of Shakespeare's
   baptism is inscribed (April 25, 1564)— borne by
   the parish clerk, page 75.
Shakespeare's father and mother — his father in the
   scarlet robes of the bailiff or mayor of Stratford
   (1568).
The 12 Aldermen in scarlet robes.
Town clerk, constable, beadle; Walter Roche, schoolmaster at Stratford (1569–70); Henry Heicroft,
   clergyman of Stratford Church (1569–70);
   William Higges, curate; Thomas Hunt, schoolmaster (1571); Thomas Jenkins, schoolmaster
   (c. 1577).

Tradition.

A group of Stratford people on the way to Kenilworth
(1575)—among them Shakespeare a boy of 11,
his father, mother, brothers Gilbert, Richard and
Edmund; and his sisters, Anna and Joan.

SHAKESPEARE'S WARWICKSHIRE CONTEMPORARIES

Michael Drayton at the
   age of 25
Sir Thomas Lucy [1]
Thomas Somerville [2]
Edward Arden [3]

Edmund Neville [4]
Sir Francis Throgmor-
   ton [5]
Fulke Greville [6]
Sir William Clopton [7]

Tradition.

THE BIDFORD REVELLERS

[To be represented either as a group on foot, or on a
float.]

Shakespeare, a group of roistering companions, and
the host of the Falcon Inn.

[If a float is used there may be a covered frame to
suggest the front of a tavern — a small tree to the
side.　The host may stand at the door and Shake-

[1] See p. 85.
[2] Condemned to death for treason, but strangled before execution of sentence. His head was exposed on London Bridge.
[3] Executed in 1583. He was hostile to Leicester and in league with Somerville.
[4] For a long time imprisoned in the Tower.
[5] Executed in 1584 as traitor. Dragged through the streets to the Tyburn before execution.
[6] Favourite courtier and friend of Sir Philip Sidney. Shakespeare's senior by ten years. See p. 85.
[7] Died 1592. His descendant later owned New Place.

speare be lying under the tree. The companions may be grouped about as though somewhat the worse for their revels.]

Tradition.

Sir Thomas Lucy and Shakespeare — possibly two or three companions with Shakespeare.

[To be represented either on foot or on a float. If a float is used, these suggestions may be followed. Shakespeare stands before Sir Thomas Lucy for deer stealing. Two or three companions are with him, all crestfallen in appearance. They stand. Sir Thomas sits as magistrate and knight, in a chair suggesting some state, and is dressed in legal robes. His cap lies on a stand near him. In any case the slain deer should be near Shakespeare and dragged along by him if he is on foot in the procession.]

The two bondsmen for Shakespeare's marriage (1582) — one of them carrying a small roll to suggest the bond.

Shakespeare at 18 and Anne Hathaway, aged 26.

The Bishop of Worcester,

Richard Burton, rector at Stratford (c. 1585).

Large groups of attendants upon the semi-annual fair at Stratford.

Warwickshire country people.

Farmers with some of their produce, shepherds with sheep, market women, milkmaids, flower-sellers, children, etc.

Ballad singers and sellers, acrobats, jugglers, bearwards leading their bears, owners of fighting cocks carrying them in cages; country performers of *The Nine Worthies,* each on horseback and in armour, morris dancers, chimney sweeps, etc.

Town crier.

A company of strolling players.

A hunting party in scarlet coats, with horns and dogs.

A group of young Warwickshire noblemen on horseback with pages and servants in livery in attendance.

Shakespeare's London.
The Court.

COURTIERS FOR THE MIDDLE PERIOD OF ELIZABETH'S REIGN

Lord Burleigh, page 226
Lord Thomas Howard, page 226
Earl of Essex, page 223
Sir Walter Raleigh, p. 90
Sir Edward Dyer
Earl of Northumberland
Sir Francis Walsingham
Lord Melville
Lord Grey
Earl of Cumberland
Earl of Pembroke

Sir Francis Drake, page 222
Sir Thomas Perrot
Sir William Russell
Sir Thomas Cecil
Lord Darcy
Lord Sheffield
Lord Windsor
Earl of Southampton
Fulke Greville, Lord Brooke, page 85
Sir Philip Sidney, p. 227

LADIES OF THE COURT IN THE MIDDLE PERIOD

Lady Cecil	Lady Carew
Countess of Derby	Lady Alice Spencer
Countess of Pembroke, page 233	Lady Russell
	Lady Bacon
Countess of Bedford	

[This group may be enlarged as much as is desired for processions lacking men and boys.]

THE OFFICE OF THE REVELS

[From Revels documents]

OFFICERS

Master of the Revels	Clerk
Clerk Comptroller	Yeoman

Workmen and tradesmen, each with some sign of his calling, but not in his holiday attire.

Tailors	Armourers
Property makers	Buskin-makers
Haberdashers	Joiners
Painters	Coffeemakers
Porters	Wiredrawers
Mercers	Messengers
Drapers	Silkweavers
Upholsterers	Linen-drapers
Silkwomen	Milliner
Furriers	Stationer
Hunters	Feather-maker
Chandlers	Smiths

106. LORD HUNSDON, THE LATER LORD CHAMBERLAIN.

107. THOMAS SACKVILLE, LORD BUCKHURST.

108. SIR FRANCIS DRAKE.

109. GEORGE CHAPMAN.

110. LADY ARABELLA STUART.

111. JOHN STOWE.
Historian and Antiquary

112. SIR JOHN HARRINGTON.

113. SAMUEL DANIEL.

114. ROBERT DEVEREUX, EARL OF ESSEX.

115. THOMAS MIDLETON.

116. EARL OF CUMBERLAND.

Basket-makers
Bootiers
Wagon-makers
Plasterers

Deckers of the house in
  birch and ivy
Horse-shoers
Ironmongers
Apothecaries

PROCESSION OF QUEEN ELIZABETH IN 1588 — THE YEAR OF THE SPANISH ARMADA.

[From Elizabethan documents]

Knights marshall men to make room
4 Trumpeters
Pursuivant-at-arms
2 Sergeants-at-arms
　　Standard of the Dragon borne by a Knight
Noblemen's and Ambassadors' servants
Grooms of the Chamber
4 Trumpeters
　　King at Arms — Blue Mantle
　　Standard of the Greyhound borne by a Knight
Earls' and Courtiers' Servants
A Sergeant-at-arms
　　Standard of the Lion
Sergeant of the Vestry
Gentlemen of the Chapel in copes, and Children of the
　　Chapel in surplices in their midst, all singing.
　　Standard of the Rouge Dragon
Clerks of the Council
Clerks of the Privy Seal
Clerks of the Signet

Clerks of the Parliament
Doctors of Physic
Queen's Chaplains
Secretaries of the Latin and French Tongues
    Standard Rouge Crosse — banners of Cornwall
    borne by a Lord between two sergeants-at-
    arms.
Lord Mayor's chief Officers
Aldermen   Sergeants-at-arms
Master of the Revels
Master of the Rents
Knight Bachelors
Lord Chief Baron
Lord Chief Justice of the Common Pleas
Master of the Jewel House
Knights who have been Ambassadors
Gentlemen of the Privy Chamber
Gentlemen pensioners, with poll axes
    Standard — Banner of Wales
Lord Mayor of London, page 226
Principal Secretary
Controller of the Household
Treasurer of the Household
Master of requests
Agents for Venice and the estates
    Standard of Ireland borne by an Irish Earl
Barons   Viscounts
Bishops   Dukes' Second Sons
Earls' Eldest Sons   Earls

(To this list should of course be added the Queen borne in state.)

Puritan families in costume

Printers' apprentices from Stratford

Rolfe Jackson   Allan Orrian
John Rampstone   Richard Tomes
Michael Mussage

Printers, later publishers of Shakespeare's works

Richard Field
William Jaggard

Schoolmasters of note

Nicholas Udall, John Still
Richard Mulcaster.

Beggars of many fraudulent types.

Bearwards leading their bears

Tradition.

Shakespeare and his boys, the horse-holders for Burbage's theatres.

Ballad singers and sellers

Early Elizabethan dramatists who were writing about the time when Shakespeare came to London:

Christopher Marlowe   George Peele
Thomas Kyd   Thomas Lodge
Robert Greene   Thomas Nashe

Explorers:

Sir Francis Drake, p. 222   Sir John Hawkins, p. 227
Sir Walter Raleigh, p. 90   Martin Frobisher, p. 227

Writers:

[This list may be enlarged according to the number of portraits available.]

Edmund Spenser (page 97) with Gabriel Harvey, page 280

Samuel Daniel, p. 223   Michael Drayton, p. 109
William Camden, his-   John Stowe, historian,
torian   page 222

Shakespeare and the Earl of Southampton walking together in friendly discourse.

ACADEMIC FIGURES FROM OXFORD AND CAMBRIDGE

Chancellors, beadles, doctors, proctors, fellows, scholars, probationers, commoners, heads of halls, bachelors of divinity, masters and bachelors of arts, doctors of law and physic, students [all in academic gowns.]

The bellman of London [carrying a large bell and ringing it], page 54.

Tinkers with their packs — all whistling or singing, page 196.

The country gentleman in town.   Coney catchers, or confidence men, with them.

Wealthy merchants, their wives and daughters

Henslowe and Alleyn, page 96.

Shakespeare and his fellow actors:
Richard Burbage, p. 96   William Kemp, p. 131

117. EARL OF ARUNDEL.
Lord Chamberlain.

118. SIR RICHARD SALTONSTALL.
The Lord Mayor of London, 1597.

119. LORD BURLEIGH.
Queen Elizabeth's Chief Counsellor.

120. SIR JOHN HAWKINS. **121.** SIR MARTIN FROBISHER, KT.

122. ROBERT COPELAND, Printer.
Showing a gown of the
guild of printers or sta-
tioners.

123. SIR PHILIP SIDNEY.

John Lowin	William Sly
Thomas Pope	Robert Armin
William Heminge	Nathaniel Field, page 85
Thomas Condell	Augustine Phillips

Workingmen's guilds in full holiday regalia.

Chapmen or pedlars, with various brightly coloured wares in wooden trays suspended from their necks, page 297.

Shakespeare with a group of his London friends.

Christopher Mountjoy, his wife, and Mary, their daughter.

Stephen Bellott, Mountjoy's apprentice, later Mary's husband.

Figure flingers throwing numbers or letters out before them, and from these telling fortunes.

Many gallants, some on horseback.

Footboys and French lackeys in attendance upon the gallants.

Charity scholars from Oxford and Cambridge [in academic garb], begging.

Doctors of physic displaying their wares and showing as many signs as possible of quackery in their contact with people.

Sailors, English and foreign.

French and Dutch weavers, carrying some sign of their trade.

PROCESSION OF QUEEN ELIZABETH IN 1600 TO
THE MARRIAGE OF LORD HERBERT.

[All those mentioned in this list may be found in the
picture facing page 37. The list is cited from
the interpretation accompanying the picture in
the publications of the New Shakespeare Society.]

Thomas, 1st Lord Howard of Walden,
Lord High Admiral, Charles, Earl of Nottingham, in
velvet and skullcap,
George Carey, 2nd Lord Hunsdon, Lord Chamberlain,
with white wand,
George Clifford, Earl of Cumberland,
Henry Brooke, 6th Lord Cobham, Warden of the
Cinque Ports with sword of state,
Earl of Rutland,
Lord Herbert,
Earl of Worcester,
Queen Elizabeth,
Edward Russell, Earl of Bedford, or Thomas, brother
of Lord Herbert,
Lord Herbert, the bridegroom,
Countess of Bedford,
Anne Russell, the bride,
Lady Russell, mother of the bride,

If this list is carefully compared with the characters
in the picture, beginning on the left, most of them may
be identified.

ACCOUNT OF THE FUNERAL PROCESSION OF QUEEN ELIZABETH.

(From official records)

See picture facing page 36

These Persons hereafter named came in their place and order, as was appointed. Also the names of such Noblemen and Gentlemen as caryed the Standards and other Ornaments at the Funeral.

First, Knight Marshall-men, to make room.

Then followed 15 poor men.

Next 260 poor women, four and four in rank.

Then servants of Gentlemen, Esquires and Knights.

Two porters
Four trumpeters

Rose Pursuivant-at-Arms [Heralds].

Two sergeants at Armes.

The standard of the Dragon, borne by the Worshipfull Sir George Boucher.

Two Queries leading a horse, covered in black cloth.

Messengers of the Chamber.

Children of the Almonry [Place from which alms were distributed.]

Children of the Woodyard.

Children of the Scullery.

Children of the Pastry, Scalding house, and Larder.

Then followed groomes; being,

Wheat Porters	Conducts in the Bake
Coopers	house
Wine porters	Bel-ringer

Maker of spice bags
Cart-takers chosen by
  the Board
Long carts
Cart takers
Of the Almonry

Of the stable
Woodyard
Scullery
Pastry
Scalding house
Poultry

Catery [Place from which food was served]

Boyling house
Larder
Kitchin
Lawndrie
Ewerie [Where water
  jugs, towels etc., were
  provided for washing
  the hands]
Confectionary
Chaundry [Candle house]

Pitcher-house   [Where
  wine and ale were
  kept]
Pitcher-house
Buttery
Seller
Pantry
Bake-house
Counting house

Then Noblemen's and Ambassadors' servants,
And Groomes of the Chamber.
Four Trumpeters.
Blewmantle.
A Sergeant at Armes.
The standard of the Greyhound, borne by Master
Herbert, brother to the Earl of Pembroke.

YEOMEN; being

Servitors in the Hall
Cart-takers
Porters
Almonry

Herbengers
Wood-yard
Scullery
Pastry

Poultry and scalding
　house
Purveyors of the Poultry
Purveyors of the Acatrie
Stable
Boyling house
Larder
Kitchin
Ewery
Confectionary
Wafer
Purveyor of the Wax
Tallow-chandler
Chaundry

Pitcher-house
Brewers
Buttery
Purveyors
Seller
Pantry
Garneter
Bake house
Counting house
Spicery
Chamber
Robes
Wardrobe

Erles and Countesses servants
Four Trumpeters

PORTCULLIS

A Sergeant at Arms.

Standard of the Lyon, borne by M. Thomas Som-
　set.

Two equeries leading a horse, trapped with blacke
　velvet.

Sergeant of the Vestry.

Gentlemen of the Chappell in copes; having the chil-
　dren of the Chappell in the middle of their com-
　pany, in surplices, all of them singing.

CLARKES:

Deputy Clarke of the mar-
　ket

Clarkes extraordinary
Cofferer

Diet

M. Cooke for the House-
hold

Pastry

Larder

Scullery

Wood yard

Poultry

Bake house

Acatry

Stable

SERGEANTS:

Gentlemen Harbinger

Woodyard

Scullery

Pastry

Catery

Larder

Ewery

Seller

Pantry

Bake house

M. Cooke of the Kitchen

Clarkes of the Equerry

Second Clarke of the Chaundry

Third Clarke of the Chaundry

Second Clarke of the Kitchen

Third Clarke of the Kitchen

Supervisors of the Dressor

FIGURES IN THE PROCESSION FOR KING JAMES' ENTRY INTO LONDON IN 1609.

King James and His Queen, pages 153, 191

Prince Henry of Wales, page 232

Lord Harrington, his companion, page 223

Arabella Stuart, page 222

André, Bishop of Ely

Master Richard Martin [who as Sheriff of London welcomed King James in 1603].

124. EDWARD CLINTON,
EARL OF LINCOLN.

125. HENRY, PRINCE OF
WALES.
(The elder son of King
James I, who died, 1612.)

126. WILLIAM HERBERT, EARL OF PEMBROKE.

127. SIR FRANCIS BACON,
Baron Verulam and Viscount St. Albans, Lord Chancellor.
From the National Portrait Gallery.

128. JOHN, FIRST MARQUIS
OF HAMILTON.

129. MARY SIDNEY,
Countess of Pembroke

Sir Thomas Egerton [later Lord High Chancellor]
Henry Howard, Earl of Northampton
The Earl of Somerset, page 301
The Countess of Somerset, page 301
The Countess of Bedford
9 Actors from Shakespeare's company, in scarlet
    capes or cloaks, and caps, Shakespeare among
    them.
Many Puritan men and women with stern and lower-
    ing looks, John Milton among them as a boy of 8.
Many of the same social types found in earlier section
    of procession.

SHAKESPEARE AND HIS FELLOW DRAMATISTS:

Ben Jonson, page 109	Phillip Massinger
Thomas Dekker	Nathaniel Field, page 85
Thomas Heywood	Robert Daborne
Henry Chettle	Richard Brome
George Chapman,	John Day
page 222	John Marston
Francis Beaumont,	Cyril Tourneur
page 85	Thomas Middleton,
John Fletcher, page 85	page 223

Tradition.
A group at the Mermaid Tavern, p. 249.

SHAKESPEARE RETIRED TO STRATFORD

Shakespeare at 52, page 249.
His daughter, Susannah at 33, and her husband, Dr.
    Hall.

His daughter, Judith at 31, and her husband, Thomas
  Quiney.

His Stratford friends.

John Combes	John Robinson
William Combes	Hamnet Sadler
Francis Collins	Robert Whatcott
Julius Shaw	Richard Tyler
John Nashe	William Reynolds

Anthony Nashe

Shakespeare and Burbage.

Tradition.

Shakespeare, Ben Jonson, and Michael Drayton together for their " merry meeting."

The parish register closed as a sign of Shakespeare's
  death — borne by the parish clerk.

THE PROCESSION

B.

Characters in Shakespeare's Plays.

IF conditions do not admit of including in the procession all the characters of all the plays, then all those
from a selected group of plays, or selected groups of
characters from all of the plays, may be presented.
The selected group of characters from a familiar scene
in a given play has sometimes the advantage of being
easier for the spectator to recognise than the entire

group for the play: it is also of course easier to provide, because of the smaller numbers and expense. The danger to avoid is, as already indicated, the impersonation of characters not sufficiently understood, and what has been said elsewhere about explaining the rôles assumed should be applied here.

In the lists following, characters have been chosen from twenty-one of the plays with reference both to their suggestiveness of the play as a whole, and to their pictorial effectiveness in the procession.

Love's Labour's Lost

King of Navarre and Biron, Longaville, and Dumain, his attendants; Princess of France and Rosaline, Maria and Katherine, her attendants.

Read I 1, II 1, IV 1, IV 3, V.

The Nine Worthies — Holofernes, Sir Nathaniel, Moth, Costard, Don Armado.

Read Act V entire.

Comedy of Errors

Antipholus of Ephesus and Adriana his wife; Antipholus of Syracuse; Dromio of Ephesus, Dromio of Syracuse; Solinus, Duke of Ephesus; Luciana, sister of Adriana. Three merchants, the goldsmith, and the schoolmaster.

Read I and II entire.

Two Gentlemen of Verona

Valentine and Proteus; Julia, Silvia, and Lucetta, Launce and Speed; Musicians.

Read I 1, I 2, II 7, IV 2, IV 4, II 1, II 5, IV 4.

Richard III

Figures for the funeral procession of Henry VI
(1, 2); King Henry borne on the bier by attendants; Lady Anne and Gloucester, who was
afterwards Richard III; the children of Clarence;
the murderers; ghosts of those murdered by
Richard III; a herald, a priest.

Read I 2, I 4, II 2, V 3.

Romeo and Juliet

Romeo, Paris, Mercutio, Benvolio, Tybalt, and
Juliet in masks and costumes for the ball; Friar
Laurence, Juliet's nurse; Peter, servant to the
nurse.

Read I 5, II 1, II 2, II 3, II 6, III 5, V.

A Midsummer Night's Dream

Theseus and Hippolyta, Lysander and Demetrius,
Hermia and Helena; the actors in *Pyramus and
Thisbe,* Oberon and Titania; Puck and the at-
tendant fairies.

Read I 1, I 2, III 1, IV 2, VI.

The Merchant of Venice

Portia and Nerissa, the Duke of Morocco; the
Prince of Arragon, Antonio, Bassanio, and their
friends; Shylock and Jessica, Lorenzo and Laun-
celot Gobbo.

Read I, III 1, III 2, IV 1.

I and II Henry IV

King Henry IV, Prince Hal, Hotspur, Falstaff,
Poins, Bardolph, Pistol, Peto, Dame Quickly,

drawers, etc. Justice Shallow, Slender, Silence, Doll Tearsheet.

Read *I Henry IV*, I 3, II 4, III 2, IV 2.
II Henry IV, V 1–3, V 5.

Henry V

King Henry; Katherine, Princess of France; Alice, her maid; King and Queen of France; heralds; English and French nobles.

Read III 4, V 2.

The Taming of the Shrew

Sly, the tinker; the hostess of the Inn; the lord and his hunting party with horns and hounds (see picture facing page 110); the players as they would appear after travelling on the road; Katherine and Petruchio; Bianca and Lucentio; Grumio, the schoolmaster.

Read *Induction*, III 1, IV 3, IV 5, V 2.

The Merry Wives of Windsor

Falstaff, Mistress Ford and Mistress Page — their husbands; the host of the Garter Inn; Dr. Caius, and servant; Anne Page and Fenton; Shallow and Slender; Sir Hugh Evans, Dame Quickly.

Read II 1, II 2, IV 6, V.

As You Like It

Rosalind and Orlando, Celia, and Oliver, Touchstone and Audrey; Corin and Silvius, the Shepherds; Phœbe, a Shepherdess; Jacques; the vicar.

Read II 4, III 2, III 3, III 5, V 1, V 4.

Twelfth Night

Malvolio, cross-gartered; Sir Toby and Sir Andrew; Fabian, the clown; Olivia and Viola.

Read I 5, II 5, III 4, IV 2, V 1.

Julius Cæsar

Cæsar and Calpurnia; Brutus, Cassius and the other conspirators; Antony and Octavius; the tribunes; the senators; a soothsayer; two poets; Portia, wife of Brutus.

Read I 1, II 1, III 2, IV 3.

Hamlet

Hamlet, the ghost, the King and Queen, Polonius; Ophelia and Laertes; the players at their first appearance; the grave diggers.

Othello

Othello and Desdemona; Iago.

Read I 3, V 2.

King Lear

King Lear as he appeared in his later miseries; his three daughters and their husbands; Edgar, Kent, and the fool.

Read I 1, II 4, III 2, III 3, IV 6.

Macbeth

The witches; Duncan; Macbeth; Banquo and Fleance, his son; the ghost of Banquo; the English and Scotch doctors and the nurse; the porter; Lady Macbeth, as in the scene at the banquet.

Read I 3, I 5, I 6, I 7, II 2, II 3, III 1,
IV 1, V 1.

Antony and Cleopatra

> Antony and Cleopatra; Octavius; a Roman lieutenant, soothsayer, clown.

> Read III 10, III 2, III 12, III 13, IV 1.

The Tempest

> Prospero; Ferdinand and Miranda; Ariel; Caliban; Trinculo, Iris, Ceres, Juno, nymphs, reapers, harpies and other wild-looking spirits.

> Read I 2, III 1, III 2, IV 1.

The Winter's Tale

> Perdita and Florizel, the old shepherd, two shepherdesses — Mopsa and Dorcas; three carters, three neatherds, three swineherds, Autolycus; many country maidens and youths.

III

PLANS FOR GROUNDS AND ACTIVITIES

London.

THE quaintness and life of Elizabethan London can at best be only suggested; beyond this it is chiefly important not to attempt too much. A successful attempt was made recently in Earl's Court, London, where a short Elizabethan street was built up, by allowing London merchants to construct temporary shops of Tudor architecture and to sell their wares in them. The wares offered were chosen for their special appropriateness to Elizabethan shops, and all the attendants were required to wear Elizabethan costume. Taverns and places of amusement, as well as shops, were provided, and the atmosphere of the Elizabethan times was creditably maintained. The plan had a very practical value in solving the question of the expense for the buildings, and the merchants were glad of the opportunity to display their goods at a place to which such large numbers of people came daily. Whether the plan is reproduced in any complete way or not, it presents useful suggestions. Even if nothing further is attempted towards reproducing Elizabethan London, much of the spirit and life of it may be suggested by a few squarely built structures of the one room sort, used as taverns for serving Elizabethan food in Elizabethan fashion;[1] as bookshops with stalls outside; as places for exhibiting Elizabethan furniture, tapestry, etc; or as places for renting Elizabethan costumes to such spectators as desire them. The bookshops or stalls might serve a very practical purpose in providing inexpensive editions of the single plays of Shakespeare, books about Shakespeare and his age, photographs, autographs, and other authentic souvenirs of him and his time. Arrangements could undoubtedly be made with booksellers and other dealers by which such things as were not sold could be returned. There might be also a dancing school where steps in Elizabethan dances were actually taught for a small consideration, and where costumed attendants illustrated the dances. Similarly, there might be a fencing school where both exhibitions and lessons were given. For a goldsmith's shop, where jewels and various trinkets were displayed, the Elizabethan play, *Eastward Ho!* gives helpful suggestions. Various other activities, chiefly of the outdoor sort, can be used in crowds of the moderate size — beggars speaking their canter's jargon, or telling tales of being wounded soldiers or mariners, etc.; quack doctors practising in the crowd; scholars from

[1] *Tavern Setting* — Large, square table with earthen bottles, mugs and pitchers on it. Stools in different parts of the room, several around the table occupied by revellers. Drawers or waiters hurrying about. A keg of sack not far from the table. See pp. 247, 249 for suggestions as to tavern interiors. For costumes of drawers see p. 294.

Oxford and Cambridge going about begging money to finish their education; physiognomists busy telling fortunes, etc. The number might be multiplied almost indefinitely.

If the pageant is held near a stream, or in a park where a lake is available for use, one side of the water may serve as the city, and the other as the Bankside, the water itself representing the Thames. Boats already on the water may be rigged to serve as Elizabethan ferry boats, as merchantmen, or as explorers' craft; and at least one barge should be dressed for the Queen and the nobility to take their pleasure in it. A flat raft with some sort of gay canopy, and seats decorated to represent chairs of state, will serve. Park boatmen may be altered into Elizabethan watermen by Elizabethan costume; the boat-cries "Eastward Ho! Westward Ho!" etc., may be adopted. If the merchantmen or explorers' craft could have on board a few characters representing weatherbeaten sailors and full of tales of adventure, a very picturesque element would be added to the setting. Drake and his crew are the best group to present. Various others could be added.

Grounds for Stratford and the Adjoining Country.

The best time to be represented in the life of Stratford is the season of the semi-annual fair. The market place where the fair is to take place should be an open square with many small and crudely constructed stalls stationed about it and some stalls farther away in odd turns and corners. Food of various country sorts, flowers, trinkets, brightly coloured articles of clothing, are to be sold at the stalls — ribbons, kerchiefs, aprons, ruffs, etc. Any available stream may serve as the Avon and furnish pleasure boats for the people.

If any one structure is attempted, it should be one suggestive of Shakespeare's birthplace,[2] with perhaps only one room open for admission, and that furnished as fully as possible with portraits and other things of Shakesperean interest. If two structures, even of the crudest sort, are to be made, Anne Hathaway's cottage across the fields to Shottery should be the second. The kitchen is the chief room to be shown there; the thatched roof is easy to accomplish, and with proper forethought there might even be some of the old English garden flowers popular in Shakespeare's time, growing outside the door. Attendants at either house should be in Elizabethan costume, and should not only be able to speak intelligently of the places represented, but to season their talk, to some degree, with Elizabethan words and points of view.[3]

Suitable activities for Stratford would be country dances to the tabor and fife, bowling on the green, archery contests, quintain, puppet shows involving a morality play story, ballad singing and selling, acrobatic performances, juggling, etc. The sheep-shearing scene in *Winter's Tale* would fit into this setting ap-

[2] For pictures at the Stratford "birthplace," see pp. 79, 82.
[3] For illustrations of the Hathaway cottage, see p. 81.

propriately, but should be outside the market place on the green, and in the same setting, somewhat closer to houses, the *Merry Wives of Windsor* might be given with fine effect. So, also, might the scenes from *Henry IV,* elsewhere suggested, be given.

IV

PLAYS AND PARTS OF PLAYS SUITABLE FOR AMATEURS [1]

THE plays and parts of plays here suggested are all chosen with reference to their suitability for outdoor presentation, as well as for other considerations. With one exception, no tragedies are recommended to be given entire tragedy making, as a rule, too heavy a draft upon amateur powers of acting, and being especially difficult before outdoor audiences, which are likely to be restless and shifting.

Plays suitable for being given outdoors, either in full or with slight reductions, are:

Julius Cæsar, The Tempest,
The Merry Wives of Windsor,
The Taming of the Shrew,
As You Like it.
Midsummer Night's Dream.

The last two have been so frequently performed out-of-doors by amateurs that those listed earlier are more desirable; but both of them are particularly well

[1] *Henry VIII* is omitted from this list only because of the problem of authorship involved.

adapted to such presentation, being set largely out of doors and involving slight characterisation.

Parts of Plays Suitable in General for Being Given by Amateurs.

Comedy of Errors. Confusions of the twins. Acts I and II.

Romeo and Juliet. The balcony scene. Act II 1, III 2.

The Merchant of Venice. The casket scene, Act II 7. The trial scene, Act IV 1.

Henry V. The lesson in English, Act III 4.
The King woos the Princess Katherine of France.

The Taming of the Shrew. Petruchio disciplines Katherine. III 1, IV 1, IV 3, IV 5, V 2.

Julius Cæsar. The orations of Brutus and Antony. Act III 2.

Richard III. The meeting of Gloucester and Anne over the bier of King Henry. Act I 2.

Macbeth. The ghost of Banquo at the banquet. Act III 4.
The sleep-walking scene. Act V 1.

Scenes Showing the Customs of the Time.[2]

TAVERN SCENES

I Henry IV. The Boar's Head Tavern. Act II 4.

II Henry IV. The Boar's Head tavern. Act II 4.

[2] Some of these have good acting value, but all are chosen rather for their illustration of Elizabethan life than for story interest or purely dramatic possibilities.

130. TAVERN SCENE — ELIZABETHAN OR JACOBEAN.

131. A PROFESSOR AND HIS STUDENTS.

247

COUNTRY LIFE

II Henry IV.   Justice Shallow's home.   Act IV 2.

Winter's Tale.   The country road and the ballad singers.   Act IV 3.

The sheep-shearing festival.

Love's Labour's Lost.   Amateur dramatic entertainment before royalty.

The show of *The Nine Worthies,* Acts V 1, IV 2.

[Include here all lines involving either the preparation or the presentation of the show.]

Hamlet.   Professional players at court.   Act II 2.

[From " *Enter four or five players* " to " *Exit Polonius with all the players but the first.*"]

The rehearsal, Act III 2.

[From the beginning to "*Exeunt players*"]

Midsummer Night's Dream.

I 2 shows the first rehearsal; III 1 the second; IV 2, the desperate straits of the company over Bottom's disappearance; VI, the play as presented before Theseus and his court. The play is valuable, too, for the light which it throws on the duties of the Master of the Revels. For showing this the beginning of I 1 should be used in connection with V 1.

132. WILL SHAKESPEARE AND BEN JONSON AT THE
MERMAID TAVERN.

V

SUGGESTIONS FOR ROYAL ENTER-
TAINMENT [1]

A Royal Progress.

A progress by Queen Elizabeth or King James as a wordless spectacle might be given with very good effect where the grounds were ample and varied, and the audience could be seated at sufficient distance. The progress could be made the setting for a succession of country sports and semi-dramatic performances, as well as for elaborate spectacles on the water and on land. Nicholls' *Progresses and Processions of Queen Elizabeth* and *Progresses, Processions and Festivities of King James I* include accounts of many of these festivities and frequently describe them in great detail.

Where the audience is small enough for dialogue to be heard in its proper rustic setting, some of the smaller devices with which Queen Elizabeth was entertained on her progresses might be employed.

[1] With the definite aim of making Shakespeare and his plays as vivid as possible, it would seem unwise to introduce for performance plays of any length or formality by any other dramatist. What is suggested here is meant only as a part of the setting for Shakespeare's life and work.

Sidney's *Ladie of the May,* given for the Queen at Wanstead in 1578, and partly described in Chapter II of this volume[2] might be used in this connection; so also the scene between Corydon and Phillida at Elvetham in 1591; *Robin Hood* and the *Fairy Queen* given at Norwich in 1592, the rustic mock marriage given at Kenilworth in 1575, etc. In what follows some selections may be made of entertainments to be given before Queen Elizabeth, although it is obviously impossible to reproduce all of the features involved.

Outline of Entertainment Provided for the Queen At Kenilworth in 1575.

Saturday — Arrival and elaborate welcome.   Already described.[3]

Monday — The Queen hunts the deer; "hounds in chase, footmen running, horses hot in pursuit, horns blasting, valleys echoing," the deer at times in the water, a part of the chase by torchlight. On the return a dialogue in the woods between a wild man and Echo.

Tuesday — Music and dancing, musicians on the bridge, and the Queen in a barge on the water.

Wednesday — Hunting.

Thursday — A fight between bears and bandogs; fireworks and peals of guns at night. An Italian doing feats of agility, tumbling, hops, jumps, summersaults, etc.

[2] See p. 32.   [3] See pp. 34, 35, also Frontispiece.

Friday and Saturday — Bad weather and "no open shows abroad."

Sunday — Sermon, burlesque marriage in tilt yard, playing at quintain. Coventry Hock Tuesday Play performed by men from Coventry. "A play of two hours long performed at night after supper," the name not being given. A banquet with 300 dishes, a very costly masque prepared but not shown.

Monday — Hunting in the afternoon; a mermaid swims to Elizabeth on her return; Triton sounds and speaks for Neptune. The Lady of the Lake, with her nymphs on the water, presents to Elizabeth Arion riding on a dolphin 24 feet long. Arion speaks and sings. The instruments and musicians are within the dolphin.

Tuesday — Coventry men perform again.

Wednesday — Shows are prevented by bad weather.

Thursday — The Queen departs.

A Court Tournament or a tilting.

See pages 181, 182, and picture facing page 190.

Performance before the Queen of one of Shakespeare's plays.

Love's Labour's Lost is known to have been played before her and its last act offers unusually good material for an outdoor performance before royalty, although the plot interest is not strong.

Reception of the French Ambassadors Suing for Elizabeth's Hand For the Duke of Alençon.

As with the scenes in a progress, this could be attempted only as a spectacle to be watched at a distance, and where ample grounds, water, several boats which could serve as barges could be had. Large flat boats or rafts with gay awnings and decorations would be needed. Coaches also would be required and are possible to devise by skilful covering of modern carriages with cotton material of the right texture and colour. A golden yellow denim, a sateen, or cambric would be best for the royal coach and pictures of Elizabethan coaches on the Frontispiece would furnish the design for the cover.

When d'Alençon's embassy arrived in England, five hundred in all, they were met at Dover by various English lords — among them Lord Cobbaur, the Earl of Pembroke, etc. A train of carriages conveyed them from Dover to the river Thames, and from there they were taken to Somerset House, one of the stately palaces along the river near London. Afterwards they made a visit of state to Elizabeth at Whitehall Palace, going there from Somerset House by barges on the Thames, and an entertainment already described was furnished them there, of a tournament between six ladies and six gentlemen, with the ladies victorious; also another, in which d'Alençon's suit to Elizabeth was symbolised.

Entertainment Before King James.

The performance of one of Shakespeare's plays before King James would be highly appropriate. There is no definite proof that Shakespeare himself played before the King, but it seems probable that he did. Also there is full appropriateness in showing King James on a progress. See list of Shakespeare's plays suggested for amateur production.[4]

[4] See p. 246.

VI

SOME ELIZABETHAN SONGS

WHEN SAMSON WAS A TALL YOUNG MAN.

Sung to the tune of the Spanish Pavan, it was very popular in
Elizabeth's time.

When Sam-son was a tall young man, His pow'r and strength in-creas-ed then, And in the host and tribe of Dan, The Lord did bless him al-way. It chan-ced so up-on a day, As he was walking on his way, He saw a maiden fresh and gay, In Tim-nath, in Tim-nath.

COME LIVE WITH ME AND BE MY LOVE.

(Words by Christopher Marlowe, sung and parodied by Sir Hugh Evans in *Merry Wives of Windsor*).

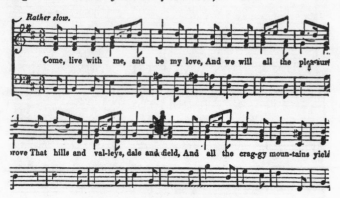

There will we sit upon the rocks,
And see the shepherds feed their flocks,
By shallow rivers, to whose falls
Melodious birds sing madrigals.

There will I make thee beds of roses,
And twine a thousand fragrant posies;
A cap of flowers, and a kirtle,
Embroider'd all with leaves of myrtle.

A gown made of the finest wool,
Which from our pretty lambs we pull;
Slippers lined choicely for the cold,
With buckles of the purest gold.

A belt of straw and ivy buds,
With coral clasps and amber studs:
And if these pleasures may thee move,
Come, live with me, and be my love.

The shepherd swains shall dance and sing,
For thy delight, each May morning;
If these delights thy mind may move,
Then live with me, and be my love.

TRIP AND GO.

(Named in *Love's Labour's Lost,* and obviously a great favourite in Shakespeare's time. The song was naturally associated
with Mayday Festivities).

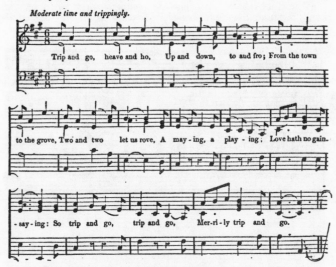

Trip and go, heave and ho, Up and down, to and fro; From the town
to the grove, Two and two let us rove, A may-ing, a play-ing; Love hath no gain-
-say-ing: So trip and go, trip and go, Mer-ri-ly trip and go.

THREE MERRY MEN WE BE.

(Named in *Twelfth Night*)

Three merry men and three merry men, And three merry men be we a,
I in the wood, and thou on the ground, And Jack sleeps in the tree.

WHEN THAT I WAS A LITTLE TINY BOY.

(The fool's song, sung as the Epilogue to *Twelfth Night*. The tune has long been used with it on the stage, although there is not proof that it is Elizabethan.)

When that I was a little tiny boy, With a heigh ho! the wind and the rain, A foolish thing was but a toy, For the rain it rain-eth ev'-ry day, With a heigh ho! the wind and the rain, And the rain it rain-eth ev'-ry day.

But when I came to man's estate
  With a heigh ho! &c.,
Gainst knaves and thieves men shut their gate,
  For the rain, &c.

But when I came, alas! to wive,
  With a heigh ho! &c.,
By swaggering I could never thrive,
  For the rain, &c.

But when I came unto my bed,
  With a heigh ho! &c.,
With toss-pots still I'd drunken head,
  For the rain, &c.

A great while ago the world begun,
  With a heigh ho! the wind and the rain;
But that is all one, our play is done,
  And we'll strive to please you every day.

DRINK TO ME ONLY WITH THINE EYES.

(Not associated with Shakespeare's Plays, but included here as one of the most beautiful of the Elizabethan lyrics. The words are by Ben Jonson, but the author of the music is unknown.)

I sent thee, late a rosy wreath,
  Not so much honouring thee,
As giving it a hope, that there
  It could not withered be;

But thou thereon didst only breathe,
  And sent'st it back to me;
Since when, it grows and smells, I
    swear,
  Not of itself, but thee.

GREENSLEEVES.

(Named in *Merry Wives of Windsor*).

I have been ready at your hand
To grant whatever you would
    crave,
I have both waged life and land,
Your love and good-will for to
    have.
        Greensleeves was all my joy,
          &c.

I bought thee kerchers to thy
    head,
That were wrought fine and gal-
    lantly,
I kept thee booth at board and
    bed,

Which cost my purse well favour-
    edly.
        Greensleeves was all my joy,
          &c.

I bought the petticoat of the best
The cloth so fine as might be,
I gave thee jewels for thy chest,
And all this cost I spent on thee.
        Greensleeves was all my joy,
          &c.

Greensleeves, now farewell, ahey!
God I pray to prosper thee!
For I am still thy lover true,
Come once again, and love me.

IT WAS A LOVER AND HIS LASS.

Between the acres of the rye,
With a hey, with a ho, with a hey,
     non ne no,
And a hey non ne, no ni no,
These pretty country fools did lie,
  In Spring time, in Spring time,
  The only pretty ring time,
  When birds do sing
  Hey ding, a ding, a ding,
  Sweet lovers love the Spring.

This carol they began that hour,
     With a hey, &c.
How that life was but a flow'r,
     In Spring time, &c.

Then, pretty lovers, take the time,
     With a hey, &c.,
For love is crowned with the prime,
     In Spring time, &c.

COBBLER'S DITTY.

From Ben Jonson's " The Case is Altered."

Troll the bowl, the nut-brown bowl,
  And here, kind mate, to thee!
Let's sing a dirge for Saint Hugh's soul,
  And down it merrily.
    Hey down a down, hey down a down,
    Hey derry, derry, down a down;
    Ho! well done, to me let come,
    Ring compass, gently joy.

VII

MUSIC AND DIRECTIONS FOR DANCES

Sellinger's Round.

THIS has already been mentioned as very popular as a maypole dance and at Christmas time in the country. It was called "The Old Hop About," and is suitable to be used in Warwickshire or London dances in a pageant.

DIRECTIONS

Old Phrasing

"Take hands and go round twice: back again, all set and turn sides: that again. Lead all in a double forward and back: that again. Two singles and a double back, set and turn single: that again. Sides all: that again. Arms all: that again. As before, as before."

In Modern Phrasing

Join hands in a circle and all go around twice. Reverse the motion and go around again once. Stop, face about, away from the centre of the circle. Repeat this. Fall into double lines and march forward. Come back. Repeat last two movements. Divide double line into two single lines and march forward. Return in double lines. Stop, face about and return in one single line. Join hands again in a circle and repeat all. Join arms in a circle.

SELLENGER'S ROUND, or THE BEGINNING OF THE WORLD.

The Canary.

The directions prescribe that a gentleman shall lead his partner to the end of the hall, and shall leave her there while he bows himself back with graceful steps, looking steadily at her. He then advances towards her, using fantastic steps, and when he has arrived, leaves as before. After he is seated, she takes the initiative, and follows the same movements he has used; then he again, etc. Six-eight time is to be used in the dance. The start should be taken on the right foot. A waltz step will serve for the advance, and the movement,— one, two, three, kick for the return.

The Hay.

A round dance especially associated with country people, and sometimes called the " farmer's dance," although popular in the city as well. It is one of the simplest of all, and involves a circle of dancers who move around, each giving the right hand and the left alternately to the next in turn until he comes to his partner again. This is one of the best dances to use for the country people of the pageant, being easy to learn, picturesque, and social in the number of participants it may include.

The Galliard.

This is danced by couples and is sometimes called the *cinquepace* because of its five steps besides the caper, or leap into the air, which comes after the fifth step. It was described in Elizabeth's time as " a swift and wandering dance." The steps are the following, with as much repetition as is desired: —

"1st step to the left
2nd step to the right
3rd step to the left
4th step to the right
5th step to the left, a leap or caper,
6th position to the left."

GALLIARD, OR CINQUEPACE.

It is danced very nimbly and gaily in triple time, being the reverse of the pavan in its abandon and the physical vigour which it suggests.

WIGMORE'S GALLIARD.

William Ballet's Lute Book, Trin. Coll., Dublin.

The Coranto.

This is a gay and rapid dance but differs from the galliard and lavolta in being a "traversing and running" rather than a dance with a caper or leap. The instructions for dancing it are these: —

> "Left foot out, right foot up,
> Right foot out, left foot up,
> Left foot out, right foot up twice."

This may be danced in lines,— either by couples or by fours; or in circles, where may be either a single circle, or one moving within another. It is effective and picturesque, and may include large numbers.

A CORANTO.

Hooper (16th Century).

The Lavolta.

The lavolta, though somewhat less common than the galliard, is like it in its quick gaiety and has even more capers or leaps. It is described in an old treatise as "rising and leaping," and this feature was sometimes introduced in alternate bars of the music. The rhyme which follows here explains that the lavolta is a round dance for two people, who take first two short steps, then a long one.

> "Yet there is one, the most delightful kind,
> A lofty jumping or a leaping round,
> Where arm in arm two dancers are entwined,
> And whirl themselves, with strict embracements bound;
> And still their feet an anaepest do sound
> An anaepest is all their music's song,
> Whose first two feet are short and third is long."

The lavolta has been called " the galliard cut short in its steps ": it may be danced still more rapidly than the galliard.   The couple dancing it put hands on each other's shoulders and, as they whirl, take first two short steps, next a long one, and finally a leap or caper.

A LAVOLTA.

THOMAS MORLEY (1563-1604).
Set by W. BYRD.

The Pavan.

A couple and two single dancers advance to music in two-four time, to the measure of eight half notes and return to the same measure.   The circuit of the room should be made two or three times during the dance.   The pavan should be danced in slow and stately fashion by the court dignitaries of the procession or play, and should form the final feature of the dancing. It is an indoor dance but may be given on a green with very picturesque effect.

A PAVAN.

(From the Fitzwilliam Virginal Book)

Thomas Tomkins (Elizabethan).

For THE SPANISH PAVAN see page 255.

AN ELIZABETHAN JIG.

This dance, for which the music is here given, was for a single
dancer. The jig was meant, as it still is, to be comic.

The Morris.

The Morris should properly be danced only by men and where large numbers take part they are apt to be in bands of six, although one dancer often danced the Morris alone in Elizabethan times, or two along a public way, or in a procession, etc. Scarfs, held out in the extended hands with a hole at each end for a thumb, were drawn across the back and add to the picturesqueness of the dance in Elizabeth's time. Handkerchiefs or sticks came to be more popular later.

The manner of dancing varied, but one form of it requires the toes to be turned up rather than pointed on the ground, and the legs to be held straight. Its simplest form is the alternately swinging forward of right foot and left, although some of the dances require a high caper. Where a band dances the leader calls the steps, but there are jig Morrises which may be danced alone as William Kemp often danced them.[1] For fuller descriptions of the Morris, see *Morris Dance Tunes,* by Cecil Sharp and H. C. McIlwaine, mentioned in the Bibliography (page 319). But it should be remembered that some of their descriptions refer to later forms of the Dance.

The Morris can be danced to the tune of *Three Merry Men,* page 257.

[1] See p. 131.

VIII

COSTUME INDEX WITH NOTES AND ILLUSTRATIONS

VIII

COSTUME INDEX WITH NOTES AND ILLUSTRATIONS [1]

THE plan of this book as a whole is to take the student of Shakespeare productions and pageants as directly back to Shakespeare's own time as possible. Following this plan, the effort has been to describe and present Elizabethan costumes as they actually were, not as one or another might find it possible to imitate them. Any other plan would prove confusing, because hardly any two groups of pageant-makers would feel equipped to do exactly the same amount towards the reproduction. Certain cautions and suggestions may be helpful towards keeping expenditures to the lowest scale consistent with success.

General plans for costuming should be made and announced by a central committee, which carries in mind not only the actual fashions of Elizabeth's day, but the artistic relation of one group of figures to another, etc. Where all the costumes are being bought, made, and paid for by such a committee, all this detail is more easily worked out, but it goes far towards solving the question of the expense of a pageant to have each in-

[1] To these notes should of course be added for reference, the chapter on *Elizabethan Dress* and such parts of the chapter on *The Queen's Revels* as bear upon the subject.

dividual pay for his or her own costume. If the wearer also assumes the responsibility for having it made, the chances for success in the pageant as a whole are much less, but adequate co-operation will solve this dilemma. It is obvious, for example, that agreement must exist as to what is Elizabethan and Jacobean, the two types of costume not differing greatly. Practical ideas should be given out too as to the ways in which the costumes are to be designed, the patterns, textures and colours, etc. No group of costumes should be considered final until passed upon by some representative of the costume committee.

MATERIALS

These must be chosen with the greatest care where means are limited, so that they may produce a general effect of richness. The caution is of especial force if the pageant or production is to occur in the daytime. Cheesecloth should be used rarely if at all. It invariably impoverishes. Sateen, canton flannels, cretonnes, cambrics, even certain broad laces, and velveteens, if bought on a co-operative basis in large quantities may be had for surprisingly low prices: so may all other materials needed. Where very large numbers are purchasing their own costumes, arrangements might be made for a central purchasing place — either a centre to which merchants would send goods sure to be needed, or one or more stores which would agree to supply the necessaries at a special rate. For the various black or red gowns needed by workingmen's guilds, lawyers, doctors, begging scholars, churchmen, etc., the material may vary from calico to sateen or silk according to the dignity of the personages represented. In many instances a modern academic gown could serve as a foundation. Fur was much used in trimming men's gowns. Where it cannot be borrowed temporarily from other uses, imitations of it may be devised. The old device of cotton batting marked with black spots lacks all pretence of subtlety, but may serve for ermine, if operated skilfully. Fur was used on men's doublets as well as on their gowns. See portrait of Lord Hunsdon, page 222, and that of Lord Buckhurst, page 222.

SUGGESTIONS FOR SPECIAL COSTUMES AND PROPERTIES

Academic dress [for Oxford and Cambridge authorities and students] — Mortarboard and other caps, gowns and hoods of various types. Heads of the university in scarlet gowns with square caps. Masters and Bachelors of Law in black gowns of light weight material, wide sleeves, square caps. Bachelors of Divinity in black gowns with hoods of changeable taffeta, square caps. Doctors of Law and Physic in scarlet gowns with hoods of changeable taffeta and square caps. Student commoners in black gowns and round black caps. See pp. 165, 247.

Aldermen — Scarlet gowns and caps. Design of these may follow general lines of those of Mayor or Lord Mayor, although materials would be less splendid.

Apprentices — Their dress probably varied more or less according to their work, although the traditional dress of

133. A FOOL'S COSTUME.

134. GABRIEL HARVEY, FRIEND OF SPENSER.

135. LEGAL COSTUME, BEFORE THE TIME OF ELIZABETH.

136. MORRIS DANCER.

137. THE UNDERPROPPING OF A RUFF.

the workingman's apprentices is a smock or a long blouse, which may or may not be belted in over somewhat loose knee trousers. Some of the plays of the time, however, suggest that apprentices in gold-smiths' shops and others where manual labour of the rougher sort was not needed, often aimed at much dandyism in their dress, especially when not at work. *Eastward Ho* illustrates this. The apprentice's cap, a round, tightly fitting one, is an important part of the traditional costume, which is the best one to adopt, browns and greys being the best colours for the dress as a whole. Where it is practicable the apprentices should be in large groups, and their songs and cheers and general gaiety should be a large feature in enlivening the procession.

Armour — A crude effect may be had by marking steel coloured cambric to represent coat of mail and even to cover specific weapons cut into proper shapes from card board or other material. If any real armour is used the two types of costume should not be brought too close together.

Beards — See portraits, pp. 85, 96, 97, 222, 223, 232. Beards were much in Elizabeth's and much importance was attached to the way they were cut. There was some tendency to associate certain fashions of wearing them with certain pursuits. A churchman might properly have his beard long; other classes affected the sharply pointed or stiletto cut and the spade. In *Midsummer Night's Dream* Bottom alludes to a fashion of dyed beards when he says of his rôle as Pyramus, " I will discharge it in either your straw colour beard, your orange-tawny beard, your purple-in-grain beard, or your French-crown colour beard, your perfect yellow." The pictures contained in this volume show a great variety.

Bellman — Long loose cloak to the knee, broad brimmed, high hat. See p. 18.

138. COURT COSTUMES.

139. VENETIAN
HOSE.

140. EXAMPLE OF THE
STOMACHER.

Bodices worn with these were not unlike the masculine doublet in outline and were equally stiff, but were somewhat more sharply pointed in front. Often extra devices, known as stomachers, were fastened to the front of the bodice and extended from the breast down upon the farthingale as in the picture on p. 282. They were especially the pretext for elaborate ornamentation, jewels, gilt and silver trimmings, etc. Sleeves were sometimes held out by large wire frames; at other times they were small like those of the doublet; and at still others, long enough to reach the ground.

Canopy for the Queen — See pictures, pp. 33 and 37.

Caps, Men's — See pp. 226, 227 (fig. 122), 232 (fig. 124), 282.

Women's — See *Women's Hats and Headdress,* and pp. 32, 152, 233.

Capes

Men's — A short semi-circular cape usually worn open in front was part of the costume. Often of velvet lined with brightly coloured silk. One type of this cape may be seen on p. 37, and others on pp. 282, 285 and 301.

Women's — Extending about half way to the ground behind. Faced with silk or velvet. Fringed.

Cassock — A long one-piece garment, usually buttoned directly down the front.

Children — See picture of Sir Walter Raleigh's son, p. 90, also p. 247 (fig. 131).

Children of the Chapel — In surplices similar to those worn in boy choirs of to-day.

Chimney sweeps — In gay gowns as women, or else in festive male attire; each different from the other and with costumes trimmed with flowers or leaves of different sorts — one with those of the broom plant; another with the woodbine; another the buttercup, etc. In each group a Jack-of-the-Green should be found in the centre. He may be all in green and must be full of nimbleness and clever tricks. The group should move most of the time in a circle, with the Jack-of-the-Green in the centre. Jumping over the broom is one of the traditional diversions of chimney sweeps on their festival days.

Churchmen — See p. 301 (fig. 165).

Cloaks

Men's — Stubbes describes them as red, white, yellow, purple, black, etc., made of cloth, silk, velvet and taffeta, of varied lengths, to the waist, the knee and even on the ground. Trimmed with lace and handsomely lined. With sleeves or without. Sometimes with hoods worn over the head and hung with points and tassels. See pp. 285, 296. The cloak of the Bellman of London, p. 54.

Clowns or fools — See pictures on pp. 280 (fig. 133), 296 (fig. 160), 300.

Commoners — *Members of the House of Commons* — In long black robes.

Constables — In striped loose fitting clothes. See picture of Dogberry and Verges, p. 191, and that of Cloth Breeches, p. 294.

Country costumes — Wealthy villagers, out of touch with the keener ambitions of the court for fashions, may have contented themselves with doublets of canvas, breeches of frieze [woolen stuff], beaver hats and for gala occasions the gowns of their guilds. Country gentlemen of any distinction of birth probably followed the courtly fashions somewhat afar off. At times some of them wore with the doublet and hose black silk gowns bordered and faced with velvet, and velvet caps to match.

Criers — Long loose cloaks to the knee. High crowned, broad brimmed hats. [The crier's duty was to declare royal and other proclamations through the city, announce certain local events of importance, etc. They may be effectively used in the pageant to cry out certain

141, 142, 143, 144.   JACOBEAN COSTUME (MEN) FOR PAGEANT

features of the procession and to announce certain activities.

Doctors (*quacks*)— Long gowns and round black caps. Large eye glasses.

Doublet — The doublet, as shown in the picture of Gabriel Harvey, was a stiff and tightly fitting garment which pointed into the waist and had a short basque-like effect or skirt below. The portrait of Southampton shows two such skirts, the two of different material, and one much longer than the other, quilted, stuffed, lined with bombazine or crinoline. At times propped with stays and made very small in the waist, " slashed, jagged, cut, carved, pincked and laced with lace of different colours." Made of very rich material and trimmed as elaborately as possible. See pp. 91, 280. The sleeves to most doublets were tight, with caps on the shoulders, although a few were puffed between the shoulders and the elbow. Many doublets were made of rich material, elaborately embroidered, trimmed with lace, or stiffened with gilt or silver trimming. See pages 37, 285.

Drawers — See pp. 247 (the standing figure) and 295 (fig. 155).

Dukes — Red velvet robes with ermine caps and small gilt crowns. Peeresses wear a similar costume, with pages to carry the trains. [These, the official robes.]

Elizabeth — Certain costumes worn by the Queen are thus described in Elizabethan records:

(1) Arched headdress of jewels and gauze, with a veil falling behind.

Black dress trimmed with lattice work of gold cords and pearly with white puffings on the shoulders and the bodice. Cut low and square at the neck which was partly covered with white network, with an ornamented black pattern on it. A device representing a phœnix rising from flames was hung by a

145, 146, 147, 148. EXAMPLES OF WOMEN'S COSTUMES (I).

149, 150, 151, 152.　EXAMPLES OF WOMEN'S COSTUMES (2).

jewelled collar from her shoulders and contained a
large diamond in the centre. Feather fan.

(2) A jewelled headdress, a gauze vest edged with spangles falling over the shoulders. The dress was cut
low and the neck covered with white and gold part-
let [wrap or covering for neck and shoulders].

(3) Flowers and pearls in her hair, close fitting black
dress, grey opaque mantle divided out behind and
passing over upper part of both arms. Ruffles at
wrist, double necklace of small pearls looped up to
the right breast. Girdle of jewels.

(4) High crowned hat. Red dress open at neck and
down front of skirt showing white kirtle (petticoat). Headdress of red silk trimmed with pearls.
White dress slashed and studded with pearls. Puffs
of white satin on the sleeves. High neck jewelled
collar. Ruffles at wrist.

Fans — See pp. 191 (fig. 103), 287, 288.

Farthingales — Most striking feature of woman's dress
throughout Shakespeare's time. Little change in early
Jacobean period. Hoopskirts and bombast or crinoline
used in abundance. See pp. 38, 191, 287, 288, 291.

Feathers — See pp. 91, 222 (fig. 106), 223 (fig. 116), 285, 291.

Footmen — See No. 3 in the picture of the funeral procession of Queen Elizabeth.

Gallants — This type admits of much variety, and as many
illustrations of it should be presented in a procession as
proves possible. Close cut beard, very elaborate ruff,
sleeves trimmed at the elbow, sword and rapier, slender
waist and broad hips are correct details. Gold spurs with
large rowels clanking in walking. Some gallants on horseback with lackeys attending on foot, chalked faces, fan,
pocket glass, long haired wigs, high corked heels, square
toed shoes, curled wig, cloaks and capes with gorgeous lin-
ings, commonplace books for writing down gleanings from

talk, etc. One or more lackeys and valets in attendance.
See p. 282, etc.

Gentlemen of the Chapel — See p. 36.

Gentlemen pensioners — See p. 33.

German ambassador.—See p. 294.

Gloves — Scented and often very elaborate. On his visit
to Oxford in 1605 King James was presented with a pair
which was decorated with a deep fringe of gold, the
upper parts being embroidered with pearls.

Hair

Men's — A variety of styles can be noted from the various
portraits in the volume, the Italian being that of short hair
cut round and curled; the French having a love lock down
to the shoulders.

Women's — Women's hair seems to have submitted to
infinite detail of arrangement. The wig, or periwig then
fashionable, was often dyed red in honour of the Queen's
hair, or of some other artificial colour which fancy dic-
tated. The hair was often built up on a wire frame or
a wicker one and was hung with jewels and pendants of
other kinds. Stubbes describes the hair as " curled frisled,
crimped, laid out in wreaths and borders from one ear to
another, propped underneath with hooks, wires, etc.; hung
with bugles, rings, other gold and silver ornaments and
those of glass."

Hats

For men — Portraits included in this volume show a great
variety of hats among the nobility and others of the
wealthy sort. The hat itself might be made of any rich
material, beaver, or merely of cloth, but it was often as
elaborately trimmed as a woman's. Stubbes explains that
where hatbands were used, many colours were affected,
the fastidious changing the colour every day. Feathers
and jewels were often used. Stubbes calls the large clus-
ters of feathers used on men's hats *coxcombs*. Shape and

153. COSTUMES OF THE WEALTHY MIDDLE CLASS.

154. A SCENE IN COURT.

size of hats varied greatly. See pp. 287, 294, 299. For countrymen's hats, see pp. 191 (fig. 102), 294, 297.

For women — See pp. 297, 301. Mary Stuart caps were much favoured. See p. 152. French hoods fitted the head closely and were made of velvet, silk, etc. Cauls, made of cloth of gold, silver, or tinsel, were even more closely fitting than the French hood. Three cornered caps like those of churchmen were also the fashions. Real hats are said to have been worn only by married women, who were expected to wear them both outdoors and in; but it is doubtful whether this rule was fully observed in either direction. The French hood of the close fitting kind was popular with both married and unmarried women, and the Italian cap, of which Melville found the Queen to be so vain, was in almost equal favour. It was similar to what is known to-day as the " Juliet cap."

Heralds — The pictures on pp. 190, 191 are a sufficient guide to most features of the dress, and to the appearance of the trumpets. White seems to have been the favourite colour for the dress. The head was usually uncovered, the arms of the sovereign and any others appropriate, being worn as in the picture. Trumpets very long and of silver were the favoured sort, and this effect may be improvised, if necessary, by enclosing the modern instrument in a longer pasteboard frame covered with silver paper, even if it is impossible to reproduce perfectly the Elizabethan shape.

Heraldic devices — These should be used in as great numbers as possible, both as banners and on the costumes of the nobility and of their retainers. Banners and other representations of the devices may be painted somewhat roughly on cambric, or on other very inexpensive material, if silk is too costly. It is impossible to include in this volume all heraldic devices which might be used, but many devices may be found on the banners over the bier

of Queen Elizabeth in the picture on p. 36, representing her
funeral procession. Her own arms, the Tudor, are shown
on the trappings of the horses there. A sketch of the
Shakespeare coat-of-arms is to be found on p. 94.

Hobby horse — See the picture on p. 173. This is devised
by setting over a man's head, to be fastened to his waist,
a small frame hung with material thick enough to hide the
lower part of his body except his feet; and furnished with
a wooden device for a horse's head in front, and another
for a horse's tail behind. The man within the frame acts
both as horse and as rider, moving the frame about with
motions as much like those of a clumsy but energetic
horse as possible.

Hose — Three favourite kinds in Stubbes's time — the
French, the " gally-hose " and the Venetian. The French
hose were round and tight fitting — the most usual fashion; the gally-hose, which were very full, extended to the
knees and were elaborately ornamented. Venetian hose
extended below the knee and were tied with silk ribands
and frequently very elaborately trimmed with lace. See
p. 282. In the reign of James I the enormous breeches
known as the *slop* became very much the fashion in upper
circles. See pp. 183, 195. They had been used throughout
Elizabeth's reign to some extent. Later in James's reign
the breeches tight at the knee but projecting far from
the waist with the aid of crinoline usurped much of the
claim to fashion, but all three styles were probably worn by
one class or another, if not by all, throughout Shakespeare's
lifetime. Bumbast, a type of crinoline, was the material
used for lining both of the fuller kinds.

Jewelry

Men's — Chiefly heavy gold chains, rings and jewels in
their hats.

Women's — Profuse amount. Gold and silver rings with

155. A SERVING MAN.

Probably a Drawer
in a Tavern.

156. VELVET BREECHES AND CLOTH
BREECHES.

Or Cityman and Countryman.

157. GERMAN COSTUMES IN THE EARLY SEVENTEENTH CENTURY.

stones, earrings, bracelets, chains of many kinds, jewelled stomachers, etc. See portraits of Queen Elizabeth *passim*.

Kirtles — Outer skirts worn over the petticoat. Apparently less bulky and less stiff than the farthingale. Much used by country women. Worn also in London, and there often of silk, or velvet, trimmed with borders of lace and fringe, etc. See pp. 287 (figs. 146, 148), 289 (fig. 151).

Knights of the Garter — The full costume involves a mantle somewhat like the Roman toga, covering the figure to the ankles, and fastened by two long cords of blue silk with silk and gold tassels. The mantle is made of blue cloth or silk, is lined with scarlet cloth, and embroidered all over with garters. It has no sleeves. The Garter of blue cloth or silk embroidered in gold with the words " Hony soit qui mal y pense." It is fastened with buckles furnished with silver bars and pendants. The hood is made of the material of the mantle. Two knights without their hoods and mantles are represented near the canopy of the Queen in the picture of her procession to the marriage of Lord Herbert, p. 37. One is the figure furthest in the forefront to the left, the other is near him.

Lady of the May — Dress of gay figured cretonne or other light cotton goods over a skirt of one colour. Tight bodice and full skirt or kirtle. Garland of flowers on her head. Nosegay in her hand. Flowers may be pinned about a dress of white.

Legal costume — Subject to some variety among the different ranks. The one here described will suffice for minor officials of the law, although any variation from it which is justified by an official portrait should be permitted. Long black robe worn open over the dress of the day. Loose sleeves reaching to the elbow. Ruff. Flat black cap with ear flaps, used at times over a white cap. Stubbes speaks of lawyers as " rustling in their silks, velvets and chains of gold," and as often attended by retinues.

This may refer either to the official gown made with as much elegance as possible, or to the dress of the city man of fashion who is also a lawyer.

Looking glasses — Carried habitually by both sexes.

Lord Chamberlain — See portrait of Lord Hunsdon, p. 222. He may wear a robe of state like that of Burleigh on p. 226 if desired. He should carry the royal sword before the Queen.

Lord of the May — Dressed in country fashion, possibly as a shepherd wearing a blouse or a forester in a green jerkin with stout knee breeches. A garland in his large round hat.

Masks — Of velvet, silk, etc. Usually black. Sometimes hiding all of the face except the eyes; at others beginning below the eyes. See page opposite.

Mayor — Lord Mayor of London — Scarlet gown. Gold chain and gold fleece attached to the symbol of the Order of the Garter. For this symbol see description under *Knights of the Garter*. He carries his own sceptre but his cap of state is carried before him. Aldermen, sometimes as many as 26, follow or precede him. Three official robes for the Lord Mayor of London — purple ribbed silk, scarlet and sable, ruby velvet barred with ermine and looped with gold. A large gold collar to which the symbol of the Order of the Garter is attached, has 28 links alternating with enamelled Tudor roses and plain gold knots.

Morris dancers — Usually nine, although the number is sometimes smaller. One or two dressed as women at times. All gaily dressed but leader most handsomely, in embroidered jerkin, gold lace, feathered hat, etc. Bells around their elbows and knees, in various sizes and tones — treble, counter tenor, etc. See p. 173.

  Robin Hood — Cap with a " magpie plume in it." Russet beard. Bells hanging in strips from garters. Coloured scarves, of light weight material and often

158. FOREIGN AMBASSADORS AT THE COURT OF QUEEN ELIZABETH.

159. WEARING A MASK.

160. A CLOWN.
Playing Pipe and Tabor.

161. AUTOLYCUS OFFERING HIS WARES (*Winter's Tale*, IV, 3).
From one of Gilbert's paintings, showing the rustic costumes of the Elizabethan period.

wide, held across the back and in outstretched hands.
Handkerchiefs sometimes used instead of scarves.

Maid Marian "in a white kyrtle withe her hair all un-
braided and blossoms in it."

Friar Tuck in a russet coat.

The fool or *dizard,* at times in a calico coat. Sometimes the leader and most gorgeously dressed of all.

The less important Dancers in white coats trimmed with
spangles.

In his *Nine Daies Wonder* already alluded to as describing his dance from London to Norwich, William Kemp
tells how as he was dancing his Morris along the
highway encountered a butcher who caught the infection of his gaiety joined him in his Morris to keep
him company to Bury. But the butcher's lungs were
not stout enough for Kemp's brisk movements so he
soon tired and parted from him. Then a maid seeing
the deserter mocked him and called to Kemp: "If
the dauncer will lend me a leash of his bells I'll venter
to treade one myle with him myself." Kemp's narrative continues:

"I lookt upon her, saw mirth in her eies, heard boldness
in her words and beheld her ready to tucke up her
russet petticoate: and I fitted her with bels, which she
merrily taking, garnisht her thicke short legs, and
with a smooth brow bad the tabur begin. The drum
strucke: forwar marcht I with my merry mayde
Marion, who shook her stout sides and footed it
merrily to Melford being a long myle. . . . She had
a good care, daunst truly and we parted friends."

Mufflers — Soft, thin, full, and light in colour, swathing the
lower part of the face.

Musicians — See p. 296 (fig. 160) for costume of piper. See
p. 190 for costumes of musicians of higher class playing in the houses of the nobility.

Neckerchiefs — Made with great care from fine lawn or cambric and variously trimmed, but apparently scorned by most in favour of the ruff.

Palisadoes — Wires supporting the hair, a part of the head-dress.

Parish register of Stratford — See picture, p. 75. [Attempt borrowing from a public library or elsewhere a book as similar to this in appearance as possible. Failing this, attempt an imitation.]

Partlets — Neckerchief, collar, ruff or other neckwear. Sometimes extending to the chest.

Pedlar — See p. 297.

Petticoats — Often of silk and bordered with fringe of a different colour.

Poking sticks — Heated sticks for pleating ruffs.

Pole axes — Axes on the end of very long poles. Halberds used by the attendants of the Swedish prince at Elizabeth's court were much the same. Both are effective for a procession and imitations may be devised so as to be carried comfortably.

Puritans — The men in short jackets, knee trousers, broad brimmed, high crowned hats, and wide white collars. The women and children in sober black dresses with white kerchiefs and caps.

Rebatoes — Stiff collars or the props for a ruff. See p. 280 (fig. 137).

Retainers of the nobility — Those of the servant class in close fitting jackets or jerkins of the colour worn by their lords. The coats-of-arms of their lords worn on their left sleeves, and at their backs. Sometimes gold chains. Distinction was naturally made between the costume of gentlemen retainers and that of yeomen.

Robin Hood — Suggestions may be taken from the hunting costumes shown in the picture on p. 110 (fig. 69), or he may be dressed with short slightly full trousers to the knees.

162. FALSTAFF AND DAME QUICKLY.

163. A YEOMAN OF THE GUARD,
Attending Queen Elizabeth on a Progress.

Stout boots, large hat. Hunting horn slung over his shoulder by a cord. Sword hanging by his side. Costume must not be too fresh, as he is a man of the woods. His men in costume similar to his.

Ruffs — They were of many sizes and varieties, occasionally showing the lowered or " falling " band, but as a rule they had much height and fulness. There must have been many men, however, who, in spite of the long continued fashion, at times eschewed the ruff for the unpleated white collar which turned back simply over the doublet. Portraits of Burbage, Lowin, Southampton, Drake, Spenser, Drayton, Ben Jonson, Nathaniel Field, etc., *passim*, illustrate that fashion. Ruffs were made of cambric, lawn, etc., and, according to Stubbes, were usually a quarter of a yard deep, although this seems a slight exaggeration. They were held up by large props or stays, see p. 280 (fig. 137), and involved many kinds of pleatings and trimmings of lace. For examples of different styles of the ruff, see page opposite, also pp. 9, 222 (fig. 110), 282, etc.

Scarfs — Worn by both sexes, but, in the allusion to be cited from Stubbes, referring only to women. He calls them " flags of pride " and says that women must, above all things, have their scarffes cast about their faces and fluttering in the wind, with great tassels at either end, of gold or silver or silk.

Scholars — Close fitting cassocks, or long garments of dark stuff. Leather girdles and leather bags. Long black cloaks may be worn over the cassocks. Costume must be decidedly shabby.

Schoolmaster — Black gown, ruff and cap or large hat. See p. 247.

Seamen — Some wearing red cassocks but most of them in jerkins and short trousers.

Serving man — See pp. 247, 295 (fig. 155).

Shepherdess — See below.

Shepherds — For the older ones, big brown or grey coats with hoods hanging from the neck. Caps and girdles. Heavy shoes. The younger ones may wear costumes suggested on p. 297.

Shoes — Usually cut low for people of rank and means. Countrymen had high heavy boots and clumsy low ones as well. See p. 294 (fig. 156).

Men's — Corked and high heeled for the ambitious in dress. Of white, black and red leather; black, white, green, and other velvet. Pantofles were low slippers worn and broad but very difficult to keep on. Pumps were also common. Bottom, in *A Midsummer Night's Dream,* orders all his fellow actors to buy new ribbons for their pumps. Rosettes were also used on men's shoes.

Women's — Same materials, corked heels, embroidery in gold or silver. Many made of velvet.

Sleeves — See pp. 282, 285, 287, 288, etc.

Stockings

Men's — Often so knit as to show open work seams down the leg. Worn with long hose of certain sorts.

Women's — Sometimes in changeable colours. Made of silk or wool.

Stomachers — See *Bodices.* See also pp. 37, 282.

Tavern setting — See p. 247 (fig. 130).

Tinsel — Material interwoven with silver threads.

Town councillors — Long mulberry coloured gowns with large beaver hats, or if these last are impossible, large black felt hats.

Trappings for horses — See the picture of the funeral procession of Queen Elizabeth, p. 36, that of the tournament, p. 190, and that of the tilting, p. 183.

Weapons — Rapiers, swords and daggers with gilded hilts. Scabbards and sheaths of velvet, etc.

Widows — Strip of white linen, with crosswise tucks in the

164. HEADGEAR FOR FOOLS' OR CLOWNS' COSTUMES.

165. CAP AND GOWN. THE UPPER HOUSE OF CONVOCATION IN SESSION.

166. THE EARL AND COUNTESS OF SOMERSET.

middle, fastened to the hair and meeting under the chin. Connected with this a kerchief of square white muslin and a veil of white or black over the head.

Witches — Rats on their heads and shoulders, ointment pots at their girdles. Bones, herbs, roots, etc., may be attached to their garments or carried by them. Spindles, timbrels resembling tambourines, and rattles are also appropriate.

Workingmen's guilds in gala dress — Long black or dull coloured gowns, often lined with fur, hoods at their backs, and heavy gold chains about their necks. Caps with long furred pieces hanging down in front. Flat square caps or large beaver hats.

Printers in gala costume — See portrait of Robert Copeland, p. 227 (fig. 122).

Yeomen of the Queen's guard — See p. 299.

Working Men — The characteristic dress of the unambitious sort in the city or the country was the short close fitting jacket known as the jerkin, with trousers slightly full at the knee, a tall, large brimmed hat, and low shoes of a simple kind. "Cloth Breeches" from Greene's *Quip for an Upstart Courtier* is a good representative of the country sort, with his blouse-like coat, his baggy trousers and his high wrinkled boots. See p. 294.

APPENDICES

APPENDICES

A. HISTORICAL EVENTS IN SHAKESPEARE'S TIME, APPROPRIATE FOR SYMBOLIC REPRESENTATION IN A PAGEANT.[1]

1 — The coming of foreign princes, or their ambassadors, to sue for Queen Elizabeth's hand.

2 — The struggle between Queen Elizabeth and Mary, Queen of Scots, and the execution of Mary, Queen of Scots.

3 — Frobisher's exploration of the coasts of Labrador and of Greenland.

4 — Sir Walter Raleigh's expedition to America and his planting of his colony in Virginia.

5 — The visit of the first Indians to England.

6 — The introduction of the use of tobacco into England.

7 — Drake's expedition into the Pacific and his wintering around the harbour of San Francisco.

8 — Drake's circumnavigation of the globe.

9 — The founding of the East India Company by London merchants.

10 — The Muscovy Company.

11 — England aiding Holland in her struggles for religious liberty. Sir Philip Sidney's death at Zutphen.

12 — The coming of the Spanish Armada and its destruction.

[1] For the first of these, Hume's *Courtship of Queen Elizabeth* recommended on p. 315 in the *Bibliography*, furnishes much information. Any extensive history of England and encyclopædias will supply information about the others.

13 — The coming of Shean O'Neill to the Court of Elizabeth
to be knighted.
14 — The Irish insurrection.
15 — The execution of Essex.

B. NON-SHAKESPEAREAN PLAYS PRESENTING
ELIZABETHAN SOCIAL TYPES AND ACTIV-
ITIES.

[Suitable for Elizabethan festivals or pageants.]

I *Shoemaker's Holiday* by Thomas Dekker.
— for understanding of workingman's life — simplicity and independence, shoemaker's shop, trade,
journeymen and apprentices — sempster's shop
— English women of lower classes.

II *Fair Maid of the West* by Middleton and Rowley.
— for tavern life of the more wholesome sort —
the explorer at home, and the breath of the new
world — an English barmaid of the better sort.

III *Four Prentices of London* by Thomas Heywood.
— for glimpses of simpler economic life of London and of middle class sense of the romantic.

IV *A Woman Killed with Kindness* by Thomas Heywood.
— for understanding of middle class domestic
conditions. A domestic tragedy based on contemporary happenings.

V *The Primer of Wakefield* — authorship uncertain
— possibly by Robert Greene.
— for village and country life, and the Elizabethan treatment of the Robin Hood tradition.

VI *Every Man in His Humour*　⎫
VII *Every Man Out of His Humour*　⎬ by Ben Jonson.

VIII *Bartholomew Fair*
> — for many types of Londoners and of London customs, all presented with exaggeration, as representing humours.

IX *Cynthia's Revels* ⎫
X *The Poetaster* ⎬ by Ben Jonson.

> — for quarrels among writers of the time.

XI *Old Wives' Tale* by George Peele.
> — Countrywoman of simple sort.

Numbers I, IV, VI, VII, IX, X and XI are available in the Mermaid editions of the works of the authors involved, published by Charles Scribner's Sons, II is in Bullen's edition of Middleton's works, V in Churton Collins's edition of *The Plays and Poems of Robert Greene,* VIII in Gifford's edition of Jonson's works or in the *Yale Studies in English Series.*

XII *Ralph Roister Doister* [2] by Nicholas Udall.
> — for schoolboys showing their pleasure in acting; also for many scenes of homely English life.

XIII *Endymion.* ⎫
XIV *Sapho and Phao* ⎬ by John Lyly.

> — for comedies written for the more refined, court audiences, and to be acted entirely by children — for allegorical allusions to the Queen and to courtiers.

XV *Arden of Feversham* — authorship uncertain.
> — for realistic presentation of a contemporary event and contemporary types. Not best suited

---

[2] XII may be found in the Temple Dramatists; XIII and XIV in Bond's edition of Lyly's works; XV in the Temple Dramatists; and XVII, XVIII, XIX and XX in any complete edition of the works of John Fletcher — Dyce's, Glover's, Bullen's, etc.

in mood and subject matter, however, for use in a pageant.

XVI   *Wit without Money* by John Fletcher.
> — for middle class life of the gayer sort, some expurgation needed.

XVII   *The Witch of Edmonton*
> — for Elizabethan belief in witches, and the life of the lower and middle classes.

XVIII   *The Woman's Prize or The Tamer Tamed* by John Fletcher.
> — is rather farce comedy than realism, being the sequel to Shakespeare's *Taming of the Shrew,* and forming an excellent choice for combination with that, by the presentation of selected scenes from each. It contains many interesting reflections of contemporary English life.

XIX   *The Pilgrim* by John Fletcher.
> — is similar in type to *The Woman's Prize* and is delightfully adapted to outdoor presentation.

XX   *The Old Wives' Tale* by George Peele.
> — is also well suited for outdoor performance by amateurs.

The following plays are equally representative of Elizabethan life but for one reason or another less available than those in the list already given, or more likely to need expurgation.

The Bellman of London.
Alarum for London.
Faire Em.
Fair Maid of Bristow.
The Roaring Girl.
The Chaste Maid in Cheapside.
The Widow of Watling Street.
The City Madam.

The Mountebank.
The Blind Beggar of Bethnal Green.
The City Gallant.
The City Wit.
Two Angry Women of Abingdon.
The Crafty Merchant.
Hard Shift for Husbands.
* Two Merry Milkmaids.
Long Meg of Westminster.
More Dissemblers Besides Women.
* The Cobbler of Queensheath.
Captain Thomas Stukeley.
The Wise Woman of Hogsden.
Tom Tiler and His Wife.
Revenge for a Father.

C. SHAKESPEARE'S PLAYS WITH FOREIGN SETTINGS.[3]

[The plays starred thus — * — are considered only partially Shakespeare's.

Ancient Rome — *Titus Andronicus,* Julius Cæsar, Antony and Cleopatra, Coriolanus.*
Ancient Greece — *Troilus and Cressida,* Timon of Athens,* Midsummer Night's Dream.*
Asia Minor (Ephesus) — *The Comedy of Errors;* (Antioch,

---

[3] Such settings for the various scenes as would distinguish one country or city from another, are thought to have been lacking, the differences being left to the imagination of the spectator, or to the playwright's descriptions.

It is to be remembered, however, that Shakespeare probably made little, if any, use of the locality-boards which were sometimes hung on the stage to state the places represented.

Tyre, Tarsus, Mytilene), *Pericles;* * (Troy), *Troilus and Cressida;* (Sicily) *Winter's Tale.*

Renaissance Italy:

Verona and Milan — *Two Gentlemen of Verona.*

Verona and Mantua — *Romeo and Juliet.*

Venice and Belmont — *The Merchant of Venice.*

Venice and Cyprus — *Othello.*

Padua — *The Taming of the Shrew; All's Well That Ends Well.*

France — *Love's Labour's Lost; Henry V; All's Well That Ends Well.*

Denmark — *Hamlet.*

Illyria — *Twelfth Night.*

Vienna — *Measure for Measure.*

Bohemia — *Winter's Tale.*

"At Sea"
"An Island" } *The Tempest.*

D. SHAKESPEARE'S PLAYS OF ENGLISH KINGS.

*Cymbeline, King Lear, Macbeth, King John, Richard II, Henry IV, Henry V, Henry VI, Richard III, Henry VIII.**

E. THE CANTER'S DICTIONARY.[4]

Anten, a church.

Anten-mart, a married woman.

Bourg, a purse.

Borde, a shilling.

Half-a-borde, sixpence.

[4] See pp. 46, 47. The dictionary is taken from a satiric Elizabethan pamphlet describing the many types of fraudulent beggars infesting London at that time. It might be useful in a Shake-

Bowse, drink.
Bowsingken, ale house.
Bene, good.
Beneship, very good.
Bufe, dog.
Bing-a waste, get you hence.
Caster, a cloak.
Commission, shirt.
Ghates, gallows.
To cly the jerke, to be whipped.
To cutt, to speak.
To cutt bene, to speak gaily.
To cutt bene whiddes, to speak good words.
To cut quier whiddes, to give evil language.
To cant, to speak.
To couch a hogshead, to lie down asleep.
Drawers, hosen.
Dudes, clothes.
Darkemans, right.
Dewse-a-vile, the country.
Drip the gigger, open the door.
Fambles, hands.
Fambling grete, a ring.
Flay, goat.
Glasiers, eyes.
Gau, month.
Gage, quart pot.
Grannam, corn.

Gube, writing.
Glymmer, fire.
Gigger, door.
Gentrymort, gentlewoman.
Gentry cofer ken, nobleman's house.
Hannan bak, constable.
Hannans, the stocks.
Heave a bough, rob a booth.
Jurke, a seal.
Ken, a house.
Lage of dudes, buck of clothes.
Libbege, a bed.
Lowre, money.
Lap, buttermilk or whey.
Libken, a house to lie in.
Lage, water.
Lightman, the day.
Mynt, gold.
A make, halfpenny.
Margery prater, hen.
Mawnding, asking.
To mill, to steal.
Mill a ken, rob a house.
Nosegent, nun.
Niggling, companying with a woman.
Pocke, meate.
Prancers, horse.
Prigging, riding.
Patrico, a priest.
Pad, a way.

speare festival as furnishing an amusing realism where beggars of the Elizabethan varieties were represented.

Quaromes, a body.
Ruffpeck, bacon.
Roger or Tif of the Buttry, a goose.
Rome i vile, London.
Rome bowse, wine.
Rome-mort, a queen.
Ruffmans, woods or bushes.
Ruffian, the Divell.
Stampes, legges.
Stampers, shoes.
Slate, a sheet.
Skew, a cup.
Salomon, the mass.

Stirling ken, a house to receive stolen goods.
Skipper, a barn.
Strommel, straw.
Smelling chete, orchard or garden.
To scowre the crampring, to wear boults.
Stalling, making or ordeyning.
Tryning, hanging.
To twore, to see.
Wyn, a penny.
Yarrun, milk.

F. FLOWERS OF SHAKESPEARE'S TIME, NAMED IN HIS PLAYS.[5]

Primrose
Cowslip
Violet
Hawthorn
Columbine
Crown imperial
Keeksies
Roses
Musk roses

Buttercup
Flower de luce
(Hemlock)
Woodbine
Rosemary
Love-in-idleness
Marigold
Rue

Daffodils
Daisy
Plaintain
Ash flowers
Hyssop
Lavender
Poppy
Marjoram

[5] A selected list.

BIBLIOGRAPHY

BIBLIOGRAPHY [1]

ELIZABETH.

Aikin, Lucy. *Memoirs of the Court of Elizabeth.* Edited by Alexander Murray. London, 1869.

Hume, Martin Andrew Sharp. *The Courtships of Queen Elizabeth. A history of the various negotiations for her marriage.* London, T. F. Unwin, 1896.

Nichols, John. *The Progresses and Public Processions of Queen Elizabeth.* New Edition, London, T. Nichols & son, 1823. 3 Vols.

Schelling, Felix Emmanuel. *The Queen's Progress, and Other Elizabethan Sketches.* Boston, Houghton Mifflin & Co., 1904. Illustrated.

ELIZABETHAN ENGLAND.

Besant, Sir Walter. *London in the Time of the Tudors.* London, A. and C. Black, 1904.

Brand, John. *Observations on the Popular Antiquities of Great Britain; illustrating the origin of our customs, ceremonies, and superstitions.* London, G. Bell & Sons, 1900–02. 3 Vols., illustrated.

Chambers, Robert. *The Book of Days.* London, W. and R. Chambers (1906?). 2 Vols. Illustrated.

[1] No comprehensive bibliography could be attempted here, the effort has been only to suggest under each topic a few of the most useful books for the reader who wishes to extend his information beyond what this volume provides. All the volumes in this list are recommended by the author.

Dekker, Thomas. *The Guls Horn-booke and the Belman of London.* Edited by O. Smeaton. New York, Dutton, 1905. [Temple edition.]

Hone, William. *Hone's Every Day Book.* With engravings by George Cruikshank. London and New York, Ward, Lock & Co., 1888.

Jusserand, Jean A. A. Jules. *The English Novel in the Time of Shakespeare.* Translated by Elizabeth Lee. London, Unwin, 1890.

Ordish, T. F. *Shakespeare's London; A Study of London in the Reign of Queen Elizabeth.* London, 1897. J. M. Dent & Co. New York, E. P. Dutton & Co.

Schelling, Felix E. *English Literature in the Time of Shakespeare.*

Schelling, Felix E. *Elizabethan Drama.* Boston, Houghton Mifflin & Co., 1908.

Sheavyn, Phœbe Anne Beale. *The Literary Profession in the Elizabethan Age.* Manchester, University Press, 1909.

Stephenson, Henry Thew. *The Elizabethan People.* New York, H. Holt & Co., 1910. Illustrated.

Stow, John. *The Survey of London.* London, J. M. Dent & Co.; New York, E. P. Dutton & Co., 1912.

Trail, Henry Duff. *Social England.* London and New York, Cassell & Co., 1901–04. 6 vols.

Wilson, John Dover, compiler. *Life in Shakespeare's England; a book of Elizabethan prose.* Cambridge, University Press, 1913. Second Edition. Illustrated.

SHAKESPEARE'S LIFE.

A. H. Thorndike } *Facts About Shakespeare.* The Macmillan Co., New York, 1912.
W. A. Nielson. }

Lee, Sidney. *A Life of William Shakespeare.* Smith, Elder & Co., London. The Macmillan Co., New York, 1916.

Wallace, Charles William. *New Shakespeare Discoveries.* *Harper's Monthly,* Vol. 120, pages 489–510, March, 1910.
Wallace, Charles William. *New Shakespeare Discoveries in Stratford-on-Avon.* New York *Sun,* May 16, 1915.
Encyclopædia Britannica. Vol. XXIV, pages 772–797.
Boaden, James. *An inquiry into the authenticity of various pictures and prints of Shakespeare. Illustrated by accurate and finished engravings by the ablest artists.* London, R. Triphock, 1824.

SHAKESPEARE'S WORKS.

Globe Edition. Edited by W. G. Clark and W. A. Wright. Cambridge and London, Macmillan & Co. New York, The Macmillan Co.
Cambridge Edition. Edited by W. A. Nielson. Boston, 1906.
Everyman's Library Edition. 3 vols. E. P. Dutton & Co. New York.
In separate volumes.
Stratford Edition. Edited by A. H. Bullen. 10 vols. Shakespeare Head Press, Stratford-on-Avon, 1904–07.
Temple Edition. Edited by I. Gollancz. 40 vols. E. P. Dutton & Co., New York, 1899–1900.
First Folio Edition. Edited by Charlotte Porter and Helen Clarke.
Tudor Edition. Edited by W. A. Neilson and A. H. Thorndike. New York, Macmillan, 1912. 40 vols.
Baker, George Peirce. *The Development of Shakespeare as a Dramatist.* New York. The Macmillan Co., 1907.

ACTORS.

Gildersleeve, Virginia Crocheron. *Government Regulation of the Elizabethan Drama.* New York. Columbia University Press, 1908. Columbia University Studies in English. Series II, Vol. IV, No. 1.

Collier, James Payne. *Memoirs of the Principal Actors in the Plays of Shakespeare.* In Shakespeare Society Publications, 1846.

THEATRES.

Lawrence, William John. *The Elizabethan Playhouse, and Other Studies.* Stratford-on-Avon, Shakespeare Head Press, 1912.

Ordish, Thomas Fairman. *Early London Theatres.* London, E. Stock, 1899.

KING JAMES I.

Nichols, John. *The Progresses, Processions and Festivities of King James the First.* London, J. B. Nichols, 1828. 4 Vols. Illustrated.

MUSIC.[2]

Armstrong, R. B. *English and Irish Instruments.* Edinboro, 1908.

Chappell, William. *Old English Popular Music.* A new edition, with preface and notes. Edited by H. Ellis Wooldridge. London, Chappell; New York, Novello, Ewer & Co., 1893. 2 Vols.

Cowling, G. H. *Music on the Shakespearean Stage.* Cambridge at the University Press, 1913.

Engel, C. *Musical Instruments.* London, 1908.

---

[2] Many of the Elizabethan musical instruments — as the sackbut, the recorder, the trumpet, etc., are treated more fully in separate volumes, but space forbids detailed reference to these here.

Galpin, Francis William. *Old English instruments of music, their history and character.* London, Methuen & Co., 1910. Illustrated.

H. C. De Lafontaine. *The King's Music.* [From the Lord Chamberlain's Records.] London, 1909.

Naylor, Edward Woodall. *Shakespeare and Music, with illustrations from music of the sixteenth and seventeenth centuries.* London, Dent, 1896. 238 pages.

Naylor, Edward Woodall. *An Elizabethan Virginal Book . . . an essay on the contents of a manuscript in the Fitz-William museum at Cambridge.* London, J. M. Dent; New York, E. P. Dutton, 1905. 220 pages, illustrated, facsims.

OUTDOOR AMUSEMENTS.

Strutt, Joseph. *The Sports and Pastimes of the People of England from the Earliest Period.* 1801. Edited by J. Charles Cox. London, Methuen & Co., 1903.

COSTUMES.

Clinch, George. *English Costume from Prehistoric Times to the End of the Eighteenth Century.* London, Methuen, 1909. Illustrated.

Douce, Francis. *Illustrations of Shakespeare and of ancient manners, with dissertations on the clowns and fools of Shakespeare.* London, Longman, 1839. Later edition, 1839. 632 pages. Illustrated.

Fairholt, Frederick William. *Costume in England.* London, G. Bell & Sons, 1896. 2 Vols. Illustrated.

Stone, Melicent. *The Bankside Costume Book for Children.* London, W. Gardner, Darton & Co., 1913.

Stubbs, Phillip. *Anatomy of Abuses. New Shakespeare Society Publications,* edited F. J. Furnivall. 1877-9.

DANCING.

Sharp, Cecil J. *Morris Dance Tunes . . . arranged for piano solo by Cecil J. Sharp and Herbert C. Macilwaine.* (New Edition.)   London, Novello & Co.

Sharp, Cecil J. *The Morris Book; with a description of dances performed by the Morrismen of England,* by Cecil J. Sharp and Herbert C. Macilwaine.   London, Novello & Co., 1913.   Illustrated.

GLOSSARY

GLOSSARY.[1]

Acatry. Place where provisions were stored.

Alderman. In earlier times the warden or governor of a guild but later a magistrate next to the mayor in dignity.

Bandore. Musical instrument like a guitar or lute. Used as a bass accompaniment for the cittern.

Barred. Striped. Possibly also *checked,* as with cross lines at right angles. Term used in describing costumes.

Bassoon. Wooden instrument furnishing the bars for the oboe.

Beadle. Official who preceded dignitaries in a procession. The university beadle carries the silver mace before the Vice-Chancellor.

Bear-ward. One having the custody and often the training of bears.

Bellman. Person employed by the city to make proclamations after first ringing his bell. In Shakespeare's time, he acted also as night watchman.

Bootier. Dealer in boots and possibly a manufacturer of them.

Burgess. Citizen of a borough, district or city. Often the official representative of one of these in Parliament.

---

[1] The author cannot hope to escape the charge of the proverbial ineptitude of makers of glossaries, for the somewhat miscellaneous group for whom the book is intended make it necessary to explain various words doubtless clear enough to some who may see them; and it may be true that words seeming necessary to some are omitted. A few of the more archaic words appearing in the text can not be authoritatively defined, so that their meaning may be inferred only from the context in which they appear.

Buck. A wash tub. A "buck of clothes" [see page 311] was a tubful of clothes or enough to fill a tub at a washing.

Busk. A corset or the stiff material extending down the front of it.

Carcanet. Ornamental collar or necklace. Usually of gold set with jewels.

Catery. Place where food is provided and from which it is served.

Chamberer. A gentleman in attendance upon the chamber of a sovereign, a nobleman, or some other person of state.

Chamberlain. A mere chamberer; also a much more important functionary. In Elizabeth's time the Lord Chamberlain was not only in charge of the chambers and officers of the royal household, but the supervisor of much of the court entertainment, and in authority over the Master of the Revels. He had much authority, too, in arranging public processions and other state ceremonies.

Chancellor. Ruling officer of a university. At Oxford and Cambridge the chief duties of the office fall upon the Vice-Chancellor, the position of the Chancellor being largely an honourary one.

Chandler. A maker of candles.

Cittern. Instrument resembling a guitar, but provided with wire strings and played with a quill or plectrum.

Clerk of the Signet. The guardian of the Royal Seal, which was put on important state documents. See *Privy Seal.*

Clowt. Cloth, clothes, torn cloth, patch, etc.

Commoner. (1) A member of the Court of the Common Council in London; (2) a member of the House of Commons; (3) a student at Oxford or Cambridge who took his food at the general tables and at his own cost.

Comptroller. An official, in public or academic organisations, to examine accounts and otherwise supervise financial business. Cf. *Treasurer.*

Common Place Bar. The court where ordinary criminals and suits were presented.

Common Pleas. A term used at times for the court itself, that is, the Common Place Bar, but actually designating the cases presented there.

Crosslet. A small cross, worn as an ornament.

Debenture. A business document or paper, showing that a certain debt was due its possessor, and marketable at such discount as proved necessary.

Deve. Due.

Estate. Used occasionally in the sense of *state,* or court formality.

Ewery. Room where ewers or pitchers with large spouts were kept with towels for washing the hands. Sometimes also a place where table linen was kept.

Farthingale. Huge skirts held out by hoops.

Fellows. In Elizabeth's time, members of a college who had a voice in its administration. Forming the academic corporation along with its Provost or other head.

Forestocks. The front parts of sleeves.

Fusles. The word seems derived from one meaning to intoxicate or confuse. Sometimes it is used jocularly in regard to some feminine extravagances or absurdities in dress.

Frislet. A small ruffle.

Gard. A trimming and often a border, of lace, silk, velvet or other ornamental stuff.

Garded. Trimmed, either with a border or otherwise.

Garniter. A person having the supervision of a granary or store of salt.

Great Seal. The highest official endorsement by the crown. See *Privy Seal.*

Harbinger. (Gentleman harbinger.) Messenger of rank.

Hautboy. A wooden double reed wind instrument used as treble accompaniment for a bassoon.

Herald. A member of the royal household appointed to make royal proclamations, and to carry a message from one sovereign to another. Prominent in official court functions, processions, tournaments, etc. In tournaments they brought challenges and mustered the combatants. The College of Heralds had the awarding and regulation of coats-of-arms. See also *king-at-arms* and *pursuivant.*

Indented. A term which, when used in reference to costume probably served to indicate notching the goods or cutting it into points, with lace showing between the points.

Jerkin. A short, closely-fitting jacket worn especially by the working class.

Kings-at-arms. Among the heralds belonging to the College-of-Arms there were three chief kings-at-arms: (1) The Garter Chief serving for the Knights of the Garter, (2) the Clarenceux, for the territory south of the river Trent, and (3) the Norroy for the territory north of the Trent. Lesser kings-at-arms were the Lyon for Scotland, Ulster for Ireland, etc. All these are named in the record of a state procession in the text.

Kirtle. A skirt.

Launderers. Washers of clothes, etc.

Mercers. Dealers in small merchandise.

Palisadoes. Wires supporting the hair, a part of the headdress.

Paned. Striped with material of another sort.

Partlets. Neckwear.

Pastery. Place where pastry is made.

Pensioner. Gentlemen pensioners were by orders instituted by Henry VIII as his royal bodyguard and gentlemen-at-arms. They carried, at first, spears; but apparently in Elizabeth's time, poll-axes. Lord Hunsdon was Captain of Elizabeth's band of Gentlemen Pensioners.

Pewterers. Makers of pewter articles.

Privy Seal. The sovereign's private seal which authorised the application of the Great Seal to a state document.

Poll-axes. Axes on the end of long poles. Borne by the Gentlemen Pensioners attendant on Queen Elizabeth.

Probationers. Candidates in a college for fellowships or scholarships. Admitted only on approval.

Proctors. Literally *proxies* or *deputies,* university officials representing it in law suits and the management of funds.

Poking sticks. Heated sticks for pleating ruffs.

Proparative makers. Apparently *property* makers.

Pursuivant-at-arms. A royal herald, or the herald of a nobleman.

Purveyor. Usually one who provides food for a table, a caterer, but apparently used of merchants of various sorts supplying the Revels Office.

Pusles. Apparently trifles of the toilet.

Rebatoes. Stiff collars, or props for ruffs.

Rebecks. Musical instruments which had three strings and were played with a bow.

Recorder. Musical instrument. Also a city officer who not only kept the records of important events but had the right to expect his oral declarations as to precedents, etc., to be taken without question in law suits.

Sergeant. One of the minor officers in the royal household: sometimes a civic officer. The word occurs with many specialised meanings in the accounts of processions found in this volume.

Tincle, or *Tinsel.* Material having silver threads woven into it.

Tires. Attires.

Vestry room. Robing room.

Yeoman. A gentleman attendant on a sovereign, or in the house of a nobleman, below the rank of a sergeant. The term was, of course, also used in a more general sense in application to the peasant class.

INDEX

A

Academic figures, 226, 227, 247, 279, 301
Actors, Elizabethan, 123; associated with Shakespeare, 128, 226; in Court Entertainments, 11; in Pageants, 226, 233; status in Law and Society, 125; travelling, 126
Alençon, Duke of, 8, 217, 253
Alfarache, Guzman de, 217
All for Money, 148
Alleyn, Edward, 123, 124, 138, 226; portrait, 96
All's Well that Ends Well, 310
Alman, dance, 177
Ambassadors, foreign, 217, 253, 296
Amusements, outdoor, 179, 318
Anatomie of Abuses (Stubbes) 172, 174, 193, 194, 199, 201, 204, 319
Animals, trained and baiting of, 50, 185, 189, 221, 225
Anne of Denmark, portrait, 191
Antony and Cleopatra, 239, 309
Archery, 184
Arden, Edward, 69, 219
Arden family, 71, 72
Arden of Feversham, 307
Armin, Robert, 129, 227
Arraignment of London, 48
Arran, Earl of, 217

Arundel, Earl of, 7, 216, 226
As You Like It, 131, 132, 164, 237
Audiences, Elizabethan, 120
Authorship of Shakespeare Plays, 115, 309
Autolycus, offering his wares, 297; song in *Winter's Tale,* 161

B

Bacon, Lady, 222
Bacon, Sir Francis, portrait, 233
Baiting of animals, 189
Baker, George, P. 144
Ballad, native song, 164
Bankside, 49, 51, 52, 134; bearbaiting rings, 50
Bankside Edition of Plays, 117
Barry, Mrs. 108
Bartholomew, Fair, 307
Bearbaiting rings, 50, 185, 189, 190
Beaumont, Francis, 58, 111, 153, 233; portrait of, 85
Bed in the Hathaways' Cottage, 60
Bedford, Earl of, 228
Countess of, 222, 228, 233
Beggars, 46, 225
Beggars' Dictionary, 310
Bellott, Stephen, 96, 227
"Belman of London"—title page, 54, 226

329